## 21K School
### Where Every Learner Finds Their Path

# THE PATHFINDERS

### 101 STORIES OF GRIT, GROWTH & THE FUTURE OF SCHOOLING

## VOLUME 1

**First Edition: 2025**
**ISBN:** 979-8-89724-298-6

**Published by:**
**Notion Press Media Private Limited**
No.50, Chettiyar Agaram Main Road, Vanagaram,
Chennai, Tamil Nadu - 600095
**Email:** publish@notionpress.com
**Phone:** +91 44 46315631

**Owner:** 21K School

**Cover Designed by:** Vivek Kumar
**Edited & Designed by:** Vaibhav Kulshreshtha

## Legal Disclaimer

The stories and narratives in this book are based on real-life experiences of learners at **21K School**. While every effort has been made to ensure accuracy, the accounts reflect individual journeys and personal achievements. The publisher and owner assume no responsibility for errors, inaccuracies, or omissions.

## Printed in India

For permissions, inquiries, or bulk purchases, please contact:
**Email:** publish@notionpress.com

# CONTENTS

# INDEX

# INDEX

# INDEX

# INDEX

# INDEX

# INDEX

# AUTHOR BIO

21K School is a pioneering global online school committed to revolutionising education through innovation, flexibility, and inclusivity. Established with the vision to empower learners beyond the constraints of traditional schooling, 21K School provides a dynamic, technology-driven learning environment where every student can thrive at their own pace.

With a presence in over 50 countries, 21K School offers internationally accredited curricula, cutting-edge digital learning tools, and a learner-centric approach that fosters curiosity, creativity, and critical thinking. The school's mission is encapsulated in its tagline—"Where every learner finds their path."

In The Pathfinders, Vol. 1, 21K School presents the inspiring stories of its learners—self-motivated individuals who have embraced online education to excel in academics, sports, arts, entrepreneurship, and beyond. These narratives serve as a testament to the transformative power of personalised learning in the 21st century.

Through its commitment to reimagining education, 21K School continues to shape the leaders, thinkers, and changemakers of tomorrow. This book is a reflection of its unwavering dedication to fostering excellence, adaptability, and lifelong learning in students worldwide.

For more information, visit www.21kschool.com.

# ACKNOWLEDGEMENT

Every great endeavor is driven by vision, passion, and collaboration. The Pathfinders, Vol. 1 is no exception. This book is more than just a collection of stories - it is a celebration of perseverance, self-discovery, and the limitless potential of young learners who dare to dream.

Our deepest gratitude goes to **Ms. Aruna Shetty, our Head of School**, **Ms. Vandana Khera (Head - Training & Development)** and our esteemed **Principals - Ms. Tanuja Amin (Indian School), Ms. Priya Dwivedi (Indian Senior School), Ms. Paminder Kohli (British School), and Dr. Amita Mehrotra (British Senior School) and the Academic Crew** for conceptualizing, identifying, collating and editing the success stories of the learners.

A special acknowledgment to our **Head - Academic Operations, Mr. Vaibhav Kulshreshtha**, who dedicatedly and creatively designed, and edited this book with the collective efforts of **Ms. Mary Sebastian, Ms. Shubha Dharwadkar, Mr. Rohail Qamar, Ms. Pallabi Samaddar, Ms. Sutripti Sourabh, Mr. Vivek Kumar,  and Mr. Mohd. Kashif**, has transformed an idea into reality, ensuring that each story is told with authenticity and impact.

Most importantly, our heartfelt appreciation goes to the **learners** whose stories fill these pages. Their courage, determination, and passion inspire us all. Their journeys remind us that education is not just about acquiring knowledge - it is about exploring, creating, and forging one's own path to success.

To the **parents** and **mentors** who have stood by these young achievers, encouraging them to pursue their dreams - thank you for believing in the transformative power of education. Your support and trust in 21K School have been invaluable in shaping these remarkable journeys.

At the heart of this initiative is the unwavering vision of our **Founder & Chief Executive Officer, Mr. Yeshwanth Raj Parasmal.** His belief in the power of personalized learning and his commitment to celebrating the journeys of our learners have been the guiding force behind this book. His encouragement inspired us to bring these success stories to the world, reinforcing the idea that learning is a journey, not a destination.

As you turn these pages, we hope you find inspiration in these stories, just as we did. This is not just a book; it is a testament to the boundless opportunities that lie ahead when learning is personalized, flexible, and future-focused.

With gratitude,

**21K School**

# FOREWORD

When we founded 21K School, our vision was clear: to create a learning environment where every child has the freedom to discover their unique strengths, pursue their passions, and shape their own path to success. We envisioned a school where learning was not restricted by geography, rigid timetables, or outdated methodologies - a school where curiosity drives knowledge and every learner finds their purpose.

The Pathfinders, Vol. 1 is a reflection of that vision. It is more than a book; it is a movement - a testament to what happens when education is designed around the learner, not the other way around. These 101 inspiring stories are proof that when young minds are given the right tools, support, and flexibility, they can accomplish the extraordinary.

Each story in this book embodies the values that define 21K School - resilience, creativity, self-motivation, and an unyielding pursuit of excellence. Whether it is a young scientist making groundbreaking discoveries, an athlete competing on national stages, or an artist using technology to redefine expression, these learners remind us that education should be about possibilities, not limitations.

In today's world, learning is no longer confined to textbooks and classrooms. The future belongs to those who can adapt, innovate, and think beyond conventional boundaries. As you read these pages, I hope you feel the same sense of inspiration that I do - the belief that every learner has the potential to change the world when given the opportunity to do so.

This book is dedicated to every student who has dared to dream, every parent who has believed in their child's potential, and every educator who has nurtured young minds with passion and commitment. It is a celebration of the future - a future where education is personalized, inclusive, and limitless.

I invite you to immerse yourself in these stories, to celebrate the triumphs, and to witness the extraordinary journeys of our young Pathfinders. Their stories are a reminder that learning is not just about acquiring knowledge - it's about finding purpose, embracing challenges, and creating a life of meaning.

Welcome to The Pathfinders, Vol. 1. This is just the beginning.

**Yeshwanth Raj Parasmal**

Founder & Chief Executive Officer
21K School

# 1

# AADHYA K

## The Game of Moves and Graceful Steps

Hi, I'm Aadhya, and I love chess and Bharatnatyam. These two passions define me, shaping how I see the world and approach challenges.

**Discovering My Passions**

Chess has been a part of my life since I was three. I still remember the first time I held a chess piece - it felt like holding a tiny universe of possibilities. Over the years, I practiced relentlessly, refining my strategies and learning from every win and loss. Today, I proudly hold 15 trophies, each representing a journey of discipline and perseverance.

While chess sharpens my mind, Bharatnatyam fills my heart with creativity. This classical dance form connects me to my cultural roots, allowing me to express emotions through movement. Though mastering the intricate footwork and expressions was tough, my dedication kept me going. Performing on stage gives me a sense of pride and joy.

**Overcoming Challenges**

Balancing two demanding passions is never easy. There were days when I felt overwhelmed, especially before competitions. But my family, teachers, and mentors supported me, reminding me that setbacks are just stepping stones to success. Whether in chess or dance, mistakes taught me valuable lessons, helping me grow stronger and more resilient.

## The Future Ahead

One of my proudest moments was being nominated for the Global Kids Achievers Award for my achievements in chess. This recognition reinforced my belief that hard work pays off. Looking ahead, I aim to continue excelling in both chess and Bharatnatyam, inspiring others to follow their dreams.

To anyone chasing their passion, my advice is simple: **Never give up. Challenges will come, but if you stay determined and love what you do, success will follow.**

I'm excited for the journey ahead and all the possibilities it holds.

2

## AADIT KIRAN HAKE

# A Journey Beyond Boundaries

At the age of eight, I stood atop the summit of Chandrashila, gazing at the snow-capped Himalayas. That moment ignited my love for adventure, a passion that would shape my education and personal growth.

**Learning Beyond the Classroom**

From trekking through India's breathtaking landscapes to exploring Thailand, Cambodia, Israel, and Malaysia, travel has been my greatest teacher. Traditional schooling couldn't accommodate my passion for exploration, but the flexibility of online learning allowed me to balance both seamlessly. I embraced online education, and soon, my world expanded beyond books and classrooms.

**Overcoming Obstacles**

Trekking isn't always easy. Weather delays, exhaustion, and difficult terrains tested my endurance, but I learned the importance of perseverance. The biggest challenge came when I embarked on my first solo trek - Kedarkantha in 2022. Despite torrential rains, I pushed forward, becoming the only one to summit that month. It was a testament to resilience and determination.

## The Road Ahead

With 21K School's support, I explored skiing, scuba diving, and mountaineering while excelling academically. My interest in history and geopolitics grew during my travels, leading me to participate in six Model United Nations conferences, where I earned multiple Best Delegate awards. My education and experiences have fueled my ambition to keep exploring and learning.

As I continue my journey, I carry this belief with me: **"In every walk with nature, one receives far more than he seeks."**

I am excited to see where my path leads next.

# Aadith Bhowmick

# My Journey to Success: A Lesson in Perseverance

Hi, I'm Aadith, a Grade 4 learner from Greater Noida, India. I love karate, building with blocks, drawing, and making animations. But my greatest passion is karate, and this year, I achieved something incredible - I won a Bronze Medal at the National Karate Championship 2024!

**The Road to Victory**

Competing at a national level was both thrilling and intimidating. My journey wasn't easy - I faced setbacks like frequent illness and muscle pain from intense training. There were moments when I doubted myself, but I kept pushing forward, supported by my Sensei and my parents.

**Finding Strength**

With every challenge, I grew stronger. My Sensei's encouragement helped me refine my techniques, while my parents' unwavering support kept me motivated. My school, 21K School, played a crucial role in balancing my academics with training, allowing me to focus on my passion without stress.

## Looking Ahead

Winning that bronze medal was just the beginning. I dream of becoming a Sensei one day, inspiring young learners just as my Sensei inspired me. Through hard work, discipline, and determination, I know I can achieve anything.

To my fellow learners: **Never give up. Every challenge is a stepping stone to success. Keep pushing forward, and you'll be amazed at what you can achieve!**

4

# AADVIK SRIVASTAVA

# Math Wizard in the Making

Can you guess how many zeros are in a Centillion? I can! Hi, I'm Aadvik, a seven-year-old from Mumbai, and I hold a world record for reciting the most zeros from 10 to Centillion in just two minutes!

## A Numbers Game

From an early age, I loved numbers and patterns. Breaking this record was one of my biggest dreams, and though it seemed impossible at first, I worked hard to make it happen. I set small goals, celebrated each milestone, and practiced every day with determination.

## Overcoming Challenges

Balancing school and record-breaking practice wasn't easy, but I learned to manage my time. My teachers at 21K School supported me, ensuring I stayed on top of my studies while pursuing my goal. Their encouragement made all the difference.

## Dreaming Big

Setting this record has given me confidence to aim even higher. I want to keep learning, exploring my interests in Abacus, dancing, piano, and football, and maybe even break more records in the future!

To my friends: **Dream big! No challenge is too great if you believe in yourself and work hard.**

Every challenge is an opportunity to grow, and I'm excited for what's next!

# Aahan Dasgupta

# From Broken Bones to Boundaries

Cricket has always been more than a sport to me - it's my passion, my identity, and my biggest dream. Playing for the Under-14 Baroda team was one of the proudest moments of my life. But my journey took a drastic turn when a rare umbral bone cyst led to a complete break in my femur.

## A Sudden Setback

One moment, I was playing, running freely on the cricket field; the next, I was in excruciating pain, unable to stand. The doctors confirmed that my femur had fractured due to an undetected bone cyst. The road to recovery was not going to be easy. A surgery involving a plate, nine screws, and 56 stitches was my new reality. For the first time, I had to pause and rethink everything.

## The Road to Recovery

The weeks following the surgery were the hardest. I could barely move, and the idea of returning to cricket seemed impossible. Physiotherapy became a daily battle - simple movements that I had once taken for granted now required every ounce of strength I had. There were moments of frustration and doubt, but I held onto hope. My love for cricket was too strong to give up.

## The Support That Carried Me Through

I wasn't alone on this journey. My family became my greatest source of encouragement. My coaches constantly checked in, reminding me that setbacks are temporary. My school, 21K School, played an essential role in my comeback. The flexibility of online learning allowed me to keep up with my studies even when I was unable to leave my bed. The unwavering support from my teachers and classmates helped me stay motivated.

## Small Wins, Big Comeback

Physiotherapy sessions slowly turned into victories. First, I could bend my knee. Then, I took my first steps with crutches. Eventually, I could walk without assistance. Every milestone felt like winning a championship. After months of persistence, I was finally cleared to start light cricket training again.

## Looking Ahead

Stepping back onto the field for the first time after my recovery was an emotional moment. Though I wasn't at my peak yet, I knew that with determination and hard work, I would get there. This experience has taught me that challenges do not define us - how we respond to them does.

**My dream remains the same:** to represent India and become one of the greatest cricket players. This setback has only strengthened my resolve. I am now more focused, resilient, and determined than ever.

To anyone facing setbacks, remember this: **Strength doesn't come from what you can do; it comes from overcoming what you thought you couldn't. The road to recovery might be long, but perseverance will always lead you back to where you belong.**

# AANVI JHA

# Conquering Challenges, One Stroke at a Time

"The enemy is within you. If you can conquer it, you will succeed." My dad's words inspire me every day.

## My Journey into the Water

Hi, I'm Aanvi Jha, a Grade 4 learner living in Singapore, and swimming is my greatest passion. It started as a fun activity, but over time, it became a challenge that pushed me to become stronger, faster, and more determined.

## Achievements in the Pool

Winning 18 medals in swimming competitions across Singapore is something I am incredibly proud of. My most cherished victories came at the Warren Country Club Swimming Competition in 2024, where I won two gold medals in the 100m Breaststroke and 50m Freestyle. Another unforgettable moment was winning golds at the Singapore Life Saving Challenge in 2023, where I competed against some of the country's best swimmers.

## Overcoming the Hardships

Balancing academics and intense training was no easy task. I train three hours on weekdays and six hours on weekends, which sometimes made me feel exhausted. There were days when I struggled with self-doubt, questioning whether I could keep up. However, my father's advice reminded me that the greatest battle is always within myself.

## Support That Kept Me Going

My teachers at 21K School made sure I could balance both swimming and studies. Their structured and flexible approach to learning helped me stay focused while excelling in my passion. My family stood by me, cheering me on at every competition, reminding me that every challenge was an opportunity to grow.

## Looking Ahead

My biggest dream is to represent my country in swimming at the Olympics. I also have a growing interest in finance and hope to explore it in the future.

Through this journey, I have learned the value of discipline, resilience, and pushing beyond my limits. If I could give one piece of advice, it would be this: **Never give up, no matter how hard the challenge seems. If you believe in yourself, success will always follow.**

The best victories are the ones you fight hardest for, and I am excited for the challenges ahead!

**7**

# AARAV ARORA

# Finding Confidence in Curiosity

## The Struggle with Learning

Hello, I'm Aarav Arora, an eighth-grader from Gurgaon, India. Growing up, I struggled to focus in long classes and felt hesitant to ask for help. It was frustrating to feel left behind while others seemed to manage effortlessly.

## A New Way to Learn

Things changed when I joined 21K School. The personalized learning approach helped me understand subjects better. My teachers encouraged me to speak up, and step by step, my confidence grew.

## Exploring New Interests

Beyond academics, I discovered a love for music and cricket. Playing the keyboard became my escape, while cricket filled me with energy. I also developed a curiosity for animals, spending time with pets and birds in my community.

## Achievements Along the Way

Through school events like JAM (Just A Minute) and the Talent Show, I overcame my fear of public speaking. Winning the Star Performer Award and the Annual Proficiency Award made me realize how far I had come.

## Looking Ahead

With my newfound confidence, I'm eager to explore more opportunities. Learning excites me now, and I look forward to new challenges.

To my fellow learners: **Believe in yourself and keep pushing forward!**

# 8

## Aarohi Narendran

# From Inspiration to Triumph: My Marathon Journey

### A Moment of Inspiration

Hi, I'm Aarohi Narendran, a Grade 4 learner from the British pathway at 21K School, currently living in Langkawi, Malaysia. I love traveling, trying new foods, and discovering new places with my family. But my greatest adventure so far has been completing a marathon - something I never imagined I could do.

### The Spark That Ignited My Journey

It all started when I watched my mom participate in a five-kilometer marathon. Standing at the finish line, I saw young kids running alongside adults, their faces filled with determination. In that moment, something changed in me. I turned to my mom and said, "I want to run next time." She smiled and said, "Then let's start training."

### The Training Begins

Training for a marathon wasn't easy. I started with short runs, slowly increasing my stamina. My mom became my running partner, encouraging me through every step. At first, I could barely run for a few minutes without feeling exhausted. But with each session, I grew stronger. I learned how to control my breathing, pace myself, and push through discomfort. Some days were tough, but I reminded myself why I started.

## Facing Challenges Head-On

There were moments of doubt, especially on days when my legs ached and I felt like giving up. But my mom always reminded me that perseverance is the key to success. The biggest challenge came on the actual race day. As I lined up with hundreds of runners, my heart pounded with excitement and nervousness. Would I be able to finish?

## The Race That Changed Everything

When the marathon began, I started strong, keeping pace with my mom. The first few kilometers felt easy, but as I reached the halfway mark, exhaustion set in. I wanted to slow down, but the cheers from the crowd and my own determination kept me going. With each step, I repeated to myself, "I can do this."

Crossing the finish line was an unforgettable moment. As I held my finisher's medal, I realized something important - strength isn't just physical, it's mental too. I had conquered my doubts and proved to myself that I could achieve anything with dedication and effort.

## What I Learned

Completing my first marathon taught me so much. I learned that discipline and consistency are essential to achieving big goals. I discovered the power of believing in myself, even when things feel impossible. Most importantly, I realized that challenges are what make victories truly meaningful.

## Looking Ahead

This experience has inspired me to keep setting new challenges for myself. I want to participate in more marathons and continue pushing my limits. Beyond running, I want to explore different sports and adventures, always staying open to new experiences.

To anyone who thinks a goal is too big or too difficult - I say go for it. You never know what you're capable of until you try. The road might be tough, but every step forward brings you closer to success.

I'm grateful to my mom for being my biggest supporter, my teachers at 21K School for their encouragement, and everyone who cheered me on. This is just the beginning of my journey, and I can't wait to see where it takes me next!

**9**

## AASTHA PATEL

# Embracing Growth and Creativity

## Discovering My Passion for Creativity

My name is Aastha Patel, and creativity has always been at the center of my world. Whether it's drawing, journaling, writing poetry, or singing, I find solace in expressing myself through art. There's something magical about bringing thoughts to life through words and melodies, allowing emotions to take shape beyond the ordinary.

## The Intersection of Passion and Ambition

Beyond the arts, I am deeply fascinated by psychology, particularly criminal psychology. The complexity of human behavior intrigues me, and I hope to explore it further in the future. Every book I read and every case study I come across fuels my curiosity, pushing me to understand the human mind's intricacies.

## My Journey of Achievements

Looking back, several accomplishments stand out, each marking a significant moment in my journey. Getting into college was a huge step - it reinforced my belief that I was on the right path, no matter how challenging it seemed. Participating in AGT (Auroiets Got Talent) was another defining milestone. Singing in front of an audience taught me to embrace vulnerability and conquer fear. Writing and producing a play for college helped me develop a deeper understanding of different perspectives, and the National Level Debate competition instilled in me the value of preparation and humility.

## Overcoming Challenges Along the Way

Despite these successes, I have faced my fair share of challenges. Balancing my interests - studying, creating, debating, and running a business - often feels like juggling too many things at once. It's easy to feel overwhelmed and unsure about where to prioritize my time and energy. However, I've learned that it's okay not to have everything figured out all at once. Growth is a journey, and I've learned to embrace its unpredictability.

## Finding Strength in Support

To manage these challenges, I have learned the importance of setting boundaries and practicing self-care. Taking breaks, asking for help when needed, and trusting my support system have all played a significant role in my journey. My family, friends, and mentors have been my pillars of strength, constantly reminding me that it's okay to take things one step at a time.

## The Role of 21K School in My Growth

21K School has played a pivotal role in shaping me into who I am today. My facilitators, like Shivani Ma'am and Oli Ma'am, have pushed me to reach my full potential, encouraging me to step out of my comfort zone and trust in my abilities. The personalized learning approach helped me explore my academic interests while nurturing my creative side, making me feel more confident and independent.

## Looking to the Future

As I move forward, my goal is to achieve balance - not just in my career but also in my mental and physical well-being. I want to pursue my dreams while ensuring that I take care of myself and those around me. Creativity and curiosity will always be part of my journey, and I look forward to discovering new opportunities that align with my passions.

**10**

## Aayat Khalid Shaikhnag

# The Path of Strength: My Karate Journey

### A New Beginning

Hi, I'm Aayat, a Grade 3 learner from Maharashtra, India, currently living in Abu Dhabi, UAE. When I first started karate, I never imagined how much it would shape my life. At the age of eight, I took my first steps into the dojo, excited but nervous. What began as an after-school activity quickly turned into a passion that transformed me both physically and mentally.

### Breaking Barriers

Karate was challenging, especially for a beginner like me. Some techniques, like high kicks and backflips, felt nearly impossible at first. But I didn't give up. My determination to improve kept me pushing forward. It wasn't always easy, but with every training session, I grew stronger and more disciplined.

### Achievements and Milestones

Earning my Yellow and Blue Belts in the same year was a major achievement for me. Being certified by the prestigious World Headquarters in Okinawa, Japan, made it even more special. Along with the belts, I was honored with two Certificates of Achievement and two Medals of Excellence, proving that my hard work was paying off.

## Overcoming Challenges

Karate is not just about physical strength - it requires patience, perseverance, and mental toughness. There were days when training felt overwhelming, but my parents, teachers, and karate coach always encouraged me to keep going. Their belief in me made all the difference.

## The Support That Built Me

I am especially grateful to my parents for always standing by my side, ensuring that I had the opportunity to pursue my passion. My 21K School facilitator played a huge role as well - she encouraged my parents to enroll me in karate, knowing it would help me develop confidence and socialize better. That small push changed my life forever.

## Looking Ahead

As I continue my journey, my ultimate goal is to earn a Black Belt and inspire other young learners to believe in themselves. Karate has taught me discipline, focus, and resilience - qualities that will guide me throughout my life.

To all my fellow learners: **Never give up on your dreams. Every challenge is an opportunity to grow, and with determination, anything is possible.**

I am grateful for everything I've achieved so far, and I know this is just the beginning!

**11**

## ABHAY BARNABAS PULICKEL

# Chasing Dreams with Faith and Hard Work

### The Seed of a Dream

Hi, I'm Abhay Barnabas Pulickel, a Grade 4 learner from Salem, India. My love for football and cricket has shaped my journey, and my mother's words - "Dreams are like seeds. If you care for them with faith and hard work, they will grow into something beautiful" - have always motivated me.

### Achievements Along the Way

One of my proudest moments was being a Star Performer in the Lit Fest Spelling Bee. Another highlight was my football team becoming the runner-up in the AIFF league for Tamil Nadu and Karnataka. These moments proved to me that dedication brings success.

### Overcoming Doubts

Balancing football with academics wasn't easy. There were times when I wanted to quit. But my mother's encouragement and my school's flexible learning approach helped me manage both.

### Looking Ahead

My dream is to become a professional footballer while staying grounded with strong values. With faith and effort, I believe I can achieve anything.

To my fellow learners: **Never give up! Believe in yourself, and your dreams will grow!**

# ADHRIT DAS CHAKLADER

# Small Steps, Big Victories: My Journey of Growth

### Discovering My Strengths

Hi, I'm Adhrit Das, a Grade 1 learner, and my journey has been one of self-discovery and growth. I may not have a shelf full of trophies, but I've achieved something even more valuable - learning to believe in myself. Being neurodivergent means I experience challenges that others may not even think about, but every step forward has been a victory worth celebrating.

### Overcoming Daily Challenges

Simple tasks that come easily to others - like making eye contact, expressing myself, or even dressing on my own - have been hurdles I've had to work hard to overcome. But I never backed down. With patience, practice, and encouragement, I've made incredible progress. Learning to communicate better has been one of my biggest achievements. Now, I can talk more confidently with my family, teachers, and friends.

### Academic Success and Personal Growth

Earning straight As in all my subjects this year was a proud moment for me. But more than grades, I've learned to express my thoughts in class, engage in discussions, and enjoy learning without fear. I used to avoid speaking up, but now, I love sharing my ideas and asking questions.

## The Role of 21K School in My Journey

My school has played a huge part in my development. The Habits of Mind program has helped me manage my emotions, stay persistent, and approach problems with a positive mindset. My teachers encourage me to keep pushing my limits, and their support has been instrumental in my success.

## Looking to the Future

I know I still have a long way to go, but I'm excited for the journey ahead. Every small achievement motivates me to aim higher. I believe that no matter how small the victory, it deserves to be celebrated.

To anyone struggling, I want to say: **You are stronger than you think. Keep going, and never stop believing in yourself!**

**13**

## ADITI AJIT

# Unleashing Potential: My Path to Success

### Finding My Passion

Hi, I'm Aditi Ajit, a Grade 4 learner from Hyderabad, India. I love painting, sketching, digital design, and playing the Kalimba. Science excites me, and experimenting with new ideas fuels my curiosity. But my journey hasn't always been easy - I had to learn how to balance my passions with academics and overcome self-doubt.

### Overcoming Procrastination and Self-Doubt

One of my biggest struggles was procrastination. I would put things off until the last minute, only to feel overwhelmed later. It took time, but I learned to manage my time better. By breaking big tasks into smaller ones and following a structured plan, I was able to stay on track without stress.

### Achievements and Learning Along the Way

Winning competitions and seeing my artwork appreciated has been fulfilling. But more than external rewards, my biggest success has been learning the value of perseverance. Whether it was completing a difficult science experiment or improving my Kalimba skills, each challenge taught me something new about myself.

## The Role of 21K School

My school's interactive and engaging approach to learning helped me grow. The flexibility allowed me to explore my interests while excelling academically. My teachers and facilitators were always there to guide and encourage me.

## Looking to the Future

I now understand that every challenge is an opportunity in disguise. As I move forward, I aim to keep learning, growing, and pushing my limits. To anyone feeling stuck, remember: **Every step you take brings you closer to your dreams. Keep moving forward, and you'll get there!**

# Aditya Vikram

# Striking Chords and Winning Games: My Path to Diplomacy

## A Passion for Music and Sports

Hi, I'm Aditya Vikram, a passionate learner from Bangalore, India, studying at 21K School. From a young age, I found myself drawn to music and sports, each teaching me discipline and perseverance in its own way. My father gifted me a toy keyboard when I was six, sparking my love for music. Soon after, he introduced me to table tennis, setting me on the path to a sport I would grow to love.

## Achievements and Milestones

Music became an essential part of my life, leading me to achieve the highest certification - Grade 8 from Trinity College London. At the same time, I worked hard in table tennis, winning the Vidyaranyapura Sports Habba Bangalore Zonal tournament in the Table Tennis U13 Boys Category. These accomplishments taught me that effort and consistency lead to success.

## Overcoming Obstacles

There were challenges along the way - nervousness before exams, noisy environments during music performances, and physical exhaustion after long hours of practice. But I developed strategies to overcome them, staying focused and learning from every setback.

## Looking to the Future

I aspire to join the Indian Foreign Services and combine my passion for music and languages with diplomacy. 21K School has provided me with the flexibility to nurture my varied interests, ensuring that I grow in all aspects of my education.

To my fellow learners: **Believe in yourself, stay determined, and embrace challenges as learning opportunities.**

# Agamjot Singh Dahella

# A Journey of Confidence and Leadership

**Overcoming My Greatest Fear**

I'm Agamjot Singh Dahella, a Grade 11 learner at 21K School from Düsseldorf, Germany. Growing up, I struggled with stuttering, which made speaking in public a nightmare. It affected my confidence, holding me back from expressing my ideas freely.

**Finding My Strengths**

I knew I had to face my fears head-on. I practiced speaking in front of a mirror, joined debates, and slowly built my confidence. Music played a huge role in my growth - I play multiple instruments, including the guitar and harmonium, which helped me develop focus and discipline.

**Achievements That Changed Everything**

One of my proudest moments was being elected CEO of Apple House in my school's learner council elections. It was a turning point that proved I could lead and inspire others despite my past struggles. Additionally, I honed my programming skills, preparing for a future where technology and leadership intersect.

**Looking Ahead**

I want to use my leadership skills and technical knowledge to create a positive impact, possibly in business or technology. My journey has taught me that persistence and hard work pay off.

To those facing obstacles: **Never let your fears define you. Keep pushing forward, and success will follow!**

**16**

## AHMED K. M. R.

# A Journey of Growth: From Challenges to Achievements

### A Passion for Learning

Hi, I'm Ahmed, a Grade 11 learner with an insatiable curiosity for the world around me. From chemistry and biology to history and mathematics, I am constantly exploring new fields, driven by a desire to understand the intricate designs of God's creations. Along with my academic pursuits, I dedicate time to studying the Quran, which strengthens my faith and shapes my perspective on life.

### Exploring the World Beyond Books

Academics have always been important to me, but I also believe in the power of real-world experiences. I play football every evening, staying active while building teamwork skills. My modest telescope offers glimpses of celestial wonders like Saturn, reminding me of the beauty of the universe.

### Achievements and Recognitions

Scoring 91% in my 10th board exams was a proud moment, reaffirming my ability to set and achieve goals. Another turning point was receiving the "Diplomatic Special Mention" at the MUN 2024-2025 conference, where I honed my public speaking skills and deepened my understanding of global geopolitics. I also had the privilege of hosting sessions on agricultural climatology and engaging with experts like Professor Radhakant Padhi.

## Overcoming Challenges

Despite my successes, I struggled with procrastination and over-reliance on technology. I often delayed tasks like revision and assignments, which caused unnecessary stress. My dependence on AI tools diminished my creativity, and poor time management affected my well-being.

## Strategies for Success

To overcome these obstacles, I implemented several strategies. I created a structured schedule, prioritizing academics, hobbies, and rest. I started waking up at 5 AM, which helped me start my day with energy and focus. Limiting screen time and actively participating in class boosted my concentration. I also made a conscious effort to rely less on AI tools and solve problems independently, restoring my confidence.

## Looking to the Future

My goal is to continue growing both academically and spiritually. I aspire to become a scholar in Islam while pursuing a career in research or teaching. With perseverance, time management, and faith, I am confident that I can overcome any challenges and achieve my aspirations.

To my fellow learners: **Discipline and focus are the keys to success. Keep pushing forward, and you'll reach your dreams.**

## AIZA BINTH SHAH

# My Journey of Dreams and Determination

### Discovering My Creative Side

Hi, I'm Aiza, a seventh-grader from Bangalore, India, studying at 21K School. My story is one of creativity, perseverance, and chasing dreams. From a young age, I've been passionate about creative pursuits like vlogging, designing, editing, crocheting, and modeling. Among these, crocheting holds a special place in my heart.

### Turning Passion into a Business

What began as a fun experiment with colorful yarn turned into a thriving online store selling handcrafted items. Running a business at my age has been both exciting and challenging, teaching me valuable lessons in time management, patience, and customer service.

### Acting: My True Calling

Beyond crafting, acting is my greatest passion. Over time, I've worked in movies, series, and advertisements, with my proudest achievement being a role in an upcoming Netflix series. I've also acted in international musical albums and ad campaigns, each project pushing me closer to my dreams.

### Balancing Academics and Passion

Juggling acting and studies wasn't easy. Offline school schedules made it difficult, but switching to 21K School changed everything. The flexible schedule allowed me to balance academics with my creative pursuits.

My teachers encouraged me to participate in public speaking, which helped me overcome nervousness and self-doubt.

## Looking Ahead

Currently, I'm working on exciting projects, including a Pan-India musical album and a Malayalam movie. I also plan to expand my crochet business and launch online classes. Each step brings new opportunities, and I'm eager to see where my journey takes me.

To my fellow learners: Challenges make you stronger. Believe in yourself, embrace the journey, and success will follow.

**18**

## AKIRA VASHISTH

# Finding Balance Through Passion

### Discovering My Love for Movement

Hi, I'm Akira Vashisth, a Grade 5 learner at 21K School, enrolled in the British Pathway. My passion for movement and focus has always been a driving force in my life. When I first ventured into yoga and dance, I was captivated by the beauty of combining discipline with creativity. Participating in events like Hindi Diwas gave me a platform to express myself confidently and connect with my cultural roots. Learning Ping Pong has also been an exciting adventure, teaching me patience and precision.

### Small Wins, Big Lessons

One of my proudest moments has been mastering new yoga poses and freestyle dance moves. These achievements hold a special place in my heart because they represent hours of dedication and the joy of seeing myself improve over time. Yoga helped me build physical strength and inner calm, while dance allowed me to unleash my creative spirit.

### Overcoming Challenges

The journey, however, wasn't always easy. Balancing yoga poses like holding my weight on one leg and perfecting intricate dance steps came with their fair share of struggles. There were moments when I felt frustrated, but I used these challenges as opportunities to grow. With daily practice and encouragement from my parents, I found my rhythm and began to enjoy the process of learning.

## The Role of 21K School

21K School played a pivotal role in my journey. The flexibility of online learning gave me the freedom to manage my time effectively, allowing me to balance academics and hobbies seamlessly. The personalized lesson plans on Century Tech made learning engaging, while innovative resources like ATL and HOM kept me motivated. Participating in school events like the Literary Fest and Reading Marathon boosted my confidence and gave me opportunities to showcase my talents.

## Looking Ahead

Through this journey, I learned the value of perseverance and the importance of enjoying the process. Every step, no matter how small, brings us closer to our goals. My love for languages has also grown, with English, Hindi, and even Japanese capturing my interest. These skills are shaping my ambitions - I aspire to become a stockbroker one day, combining discipline with analytical thinking.

To my fellow learners, my message is simple: **Never stop learning. It's okay to face challenges because they push you to grow. Embrace your mistakes, practice consistently, and remember to celebrate your small wins.**

**19**

## Amairah Khan

# The Power of Imagination: My Journey into Storytelling

**Discovering My Love for Writing**

Hi, I'm Amairah Khan, a Grade 6 learner, and my world is filled with stories waiting to be told. From a young age, I found myself drawn to books, fascinated by the way words could transport readers to different worlds. I would spend hours creating characters, imagining adventures, and writing down my own stories. Storytelling became my passion, allowing me to express my thoughts, emotions, and creativity in ways I never imagined.

**Nurturing My Passion**

At first, writing was just a hobby. I scribbled short tales in my notebooks, often too shy to share them. But as I read more books and watched inspiring authors speak about their journeys, I realized that stories have the power to connect people. That's when I decided to take writing seriously. I started participating in creative writing contests, and each experience helped me grow more confident in my abilities.

**Achievements and Growth**

One of my proudest moments was winning a storytelling competition at school. It was the first time I shared my work with a larger audience, and the positive feedback encouraged me to keep going. I also started writing a fantasy novel, a dream project that I hope to complete soon. Through this journey, I've learned that writing isn't just about words - it's about emotion, imagination, and persistence.

## Overcoming Challenges

Like any creative journey, mine had its hurdles. There were days when I struggled with self-doubt, wondering if my stories were good enough. Writer's block often left me staring at blank pages. But I learned that every writer faces these moments. I started journaling daily, reading more diverse books, and reminding myself that the best stories come from the heart. My teachers at 21K School played a huge role in encouraging me, offering valuable feedback and guiding me to improve my craft.

## Looking to the Future

My dream is to become an author, publishing books that inspire and entertain readers worldwide. I also want to explore scriptwriting, bringing stories to life on screen. The world of storytelling is vast, and I'm excited to continue my journey, learning and growing along the way.

To my fellow learners: **If you have a story inside you, don't be afraid to share it. Your words have the power to inspire, heal, and change the world. Keep writing!**

**20**

## AMARA VISRAM

# Dancing to My Own Rhythm: A Journey of Grace and Strength

### A Passion for Dance

Hi, I'm Amara Visram, a Grade 7 learner, and dancing is my language of expression. Ever since I can remember, movement has been my way of communicating emotions, telling stories, and finding joy. From ballet to contemporary, every dance form I explore brings me closer to understanding the rhythm of life.

### The Road to Excellence

Dance is not just an art; it's a discipline. Early morning rehearsals, perfecting every turn, and maintaining strength and flexibility require dedication. There were times when my feet ached from practice, but I knew that every step brought me closer to my goals. Winning first place in a citywide dance competition was one of my proudest moments, proving that perseverance pays off.

### Overcoming Challenges

Dance is physically demanding, but the biggest challenge was overcoming stage fright. Performing in front of an audience was nerve-wracking at first, but I learned to channel my fear into energy. Breathing exercises, visualization, and the support of my dance mentors helped me build confidence.

## Balancing Academics and Passion

Managing school and dance wasn't always easy, but 21K School's flexible learning schedule allowed me to dedicate time to both. My teachers encouraged my artistic pursuits while ensuring I stayed on track academically. Learning how to balance my time effectively was a lesson I will carry with me forever.

## Looking Ahead

My dream is to perform on international stages, blending different dance styles to create something unique. Dance has taught me resilience, discipline, and the power of expression, and I am excited to see where my passion takes me.

To my fellow learners: **Follow your rhythm, embrace your passion, and never be afraid to take center stage in your life.**

# 21

## ANANYA MATHUR

# Crafting My World: A Journey of Art and Exploration

### Discovering My Artistic Voice

Hi, I'm Ananya Mathur, a Grade 4 learner with a passion for art, creativity, and learning. Ever since I could hold a crayon, I have been drawn to colors and shapes, eager to bring my imagination to life. My journey into the world of art has been a wonderful adventure of self-expression, discovery, and growth.

### Achievements and Passion Projects

Winning multiple school art competitions and having my work displayed in exhibitions has been an incredible honor. My teachers at 21K School have encouraged me to explore different artistic styles, from watercolors to digital art. With every piece I create, I learn something new about technique, patience, and storytelling through visuals.

### Overcoming Challenges

Like any artist, I have faced struggles. There were times when I felt uninspired or doubted my abilities. I learned that creativity flows when you give yourself the space to experiment and make mistakes. My parents and mentors have always encouraged me to keep pushing forward, reminding me that art is a journey, not a destination.

## Looking to the Future

My dream is to become an illustrator and animator, bringing characters and worlds to life. I want to use my creativity to tell stories that inspire others. Art has taught me to see the world differently, and I hope to share my vision with others.

To my fellow learners: **Create, explore, and never be afraid to dream big!**

**22**

## ANIKA ANILKUMAR

# The Power of Words: My Journey in Public Speaking

### Finding My Voice

Hi, I'm Anika Anilkumar, a Grade 5 learner with a deep love for communication. From an early age, I loved talking to people and expressing my ideas. But it wasn't until I participated in my first speech competition that I realized the true power of words.

### Achievements and Milestones

I have won multiple speech and debate competitions, representing my school and honing my ability to think critically. Speaking in front of an audience once felt nerve-wracking, but with practice and perseverance, I found confidence in my voice.

### Overcoming Stage Fright

Public speaking wasn't always easy. I used to feel anxious before stepping onto the stage. But with guidance from my mentors and support from my school, I learned to manage my nerves. Breathing exercises and visualization techniques have helped me become a more composed and effective speaker.

### Looking to the Future

I dream of becoming a motivational speaker and writer, using my voice to inspire and educate others. My journey has taught me that communication is a powerful tool, and I want to use it to make a difference.

Your voice matters. Speak with confidence, and the world will listen!

**23**

## ANISHA PANGAONKAR

# The Journey of an Equestrian Dreamer

### Discovering My Passion for Horse Riding

Hi, I'm Anisha Pangaonkar, a Grade 5 learner who found a world of strength and freedom in horse riding. The first time I sat on a horse, I felt an instant connection. It wasn't just about riding - it was about trust, discipline, and the bond between horse and rider. I was fascinated by the grace and power of horses and knew that I wanted to learn everything about them.

### Overcoming Fear and Challenges

Horse riding isn't easy. Controlling a powerful animal requires confidence and patience. In the beginning, I struggled with balance and fear, especially after a fall during training. That moment was terrifying, and I wondered if I would ever get back on a horse again. But my passion was stronger than my fear. With perseverance and guidance from my trainers, I learned to trust my instincts and push beyond my limits. I practiced tirelessly, working on my posture, reins control, and riding techniques. Each small improvement motivated me to keep going.

### Achievements Along the Way

Winning my first equestrian competition was a defining moment. The months of training, early morning rides, and dedication paid off when I received my first medal. The feeling of crossing the finish line, hearing the applause, and knowing that I had done my best was unforgettable.

I also started learning about horse care, understanding their behaviors, and developing a deeper connection with them. My school, 21K School, supported me by giving me the flexibility to balance my academics and passion seamlessly. This allowed me to train effectively without falling behind in my studies.

## The Support That Kept Me Going

Behind every rider is a team of supporters. My parents have been my biggest cheerleaders, encouraging me through every challenge. My trainers taught me discipline and resilience, ensuring that I never gave up when things got tough. My friends also played a crucial role, always cheering me on during competitions and training sessions. The support from my school, teachers, and fellow learners made my journey even more fulfilling. They understood my commitment and always encouraged me to follow my dreams.

## Lessons Learned and Future Goals

Through this journey, I have learned that discipline and consistency are key to mastering any skill. Every time I ride, I discover something new about myself - whether it's patience, persistence, or the ability to stay calm under pressure. The connection between a rider and their horse is special, built on trust and understanding, and that has taught me the importance of forming bonds in all aspects of life.

My dream is to compete in national and international equestrian championships, proving that dedication and passion can lead to extraordinary achievements. I also want to continue educating myself about horse care and training methods to become a well-rounded equestrian. Horse riding has taught me discipline, resilience, and the power of never giving up. One day, I hope to inspire other young riders to take up this sport and experience the same joy that I do.

To my fellow learners: **Chase your passion fearlessly, and success will follow. No dream is too big when you believe in yourself and work hard to achieve it.**

# 24

## ANISHKA ROY

# My Love for Science and Innovation

### A Curious Mind

Hi, I'm Anishka Roy, a Grade 4 learner who loves exploring the world of science. From an early age, I found myself fascinated by how things work - whether it was the movement of planets, the principles of energy, or the wonders of the human body. My curiosity drives me to experiment, research, and ask endless questions. I see science as a way to unlock the mysteries of the universe, and I love every moment of exploring it.

### The Joy of Learning

At 21K School, I found an environment that nurtured my love for science. I participated in various science fairs and projects, including building a simple water purification system and creating a model to demonstrate solar energy. These experiences fueled my interest in sustainable innovations. Each project taught me the importance of observation, patience, and logical thinking.

### Challenges and Growth

Not every experiment succeeds on the first try. There were times when projects failed, but I learned that failure is a stepping stone to success. Each mistake taught me something new, pushing me to think differently and improve my methods. There were moments when I felt discouraged, but my teachers and parents always reminded me that the best scientists never stop questioning and exploring.

## Achievements and Recognition

Winning my first science fair was a defining moment in my journey. It showed me that my ideas and curiosity could lead to meaningful innovations. Presenting my project to judges and explaining my thought process gave me the confidence to pursue more complex scientific studies. The encouragement I received from my peers and mentors made me realize that I wanted to dedicate my future to science.

## The Support That Kept Me Going

Behind every young scientist is a group of supporters who believe in them. My family has been my strongest pillar, encouraging my passion and ensuring I have the resources to explore my interests. My school played a crucial role by providing me with opportunities to engage in hands-on learning and mentorship. My teachers at 21K School have inspired me to keep pushing my boundaries, guiding me toward a deeper understanding of scientific concepts.

## Looking to the Future

I dream of becoming a scientist and working on projects that help solve global challenges, especially in renewable energy. Science has the power to change lives, and I want to contribute to that future by developing sustainable solutions for a better world. My goal is to study at a top university and work on real-world scientific problems that can make a difference in people's lives.

To my fellow learners: **Stay curious, keep experimenting, and never stop asking 'why.' Science is full of endless possibilities, and with persistence, you can change the world!**

**25**

# ANJANSWAROOP G. S.

# The Art of Music and Dedication

### A Love for Music

Hi, I'm Anjanswaroop, an 8th grader who has found joy and discipline in music. The first time I played the keyboard, I knew that music would be a big part of my life. Over the years, I expanded my skills, exploring different musical styles and instruments. Whether it was classical piano, electronic beats, or soulful melodies, music became my language of self-expression.

### Dedication and Practice

Music requires patience and constant learning. Some pieces took weeks to master, but each challenge made me a better musician. I spent hours practicing daily, perfecting every note and rhythm. There were moments when I felt frustrated, but I reminded myself that every great musician once started as a beginner. Performing in school events and competitions helped me build confidence, and winning a local music contest was a proud moment.

### Overcoming Stage Fear

I used to feel nervous performing in front of a crowd. My hands would shake, and I would forget notes. But with practice and encouragement from my teachers and family, I learned to focus on the music rather than the audience. I developed techniques like deep breathing and visualization, which helped me stay calm on stage. Now, every performance feels like an opportunity to share my passion.

## Achievements and Milestones

One of my biggest achievements was composing my own piece of music. It was a mix of classical and modern elements, and performing it in front of my school was an unforgettable experience. I also participated in an inter-school band competition, where we performed as a team, learning the value of coordination and collaboration in music.

## The Role of 21K School

My school has played a crucial role in my musical journey. The flexible learning approach at 21K School allowed me to dedicate time to both my academics and my passion for music. My teachers supported my endeavors, ensuring that I could balance practice with studies. Their encouragement pushed me to participate in competitions and explore different musical techniques.

## Looking Ahead

I hope to compose my own music professionally one day and inspire others through melodies. Music has taught me discipline, creativity, and resilience - lessons that will guide me throughout life. My dream is to study music at a prestigious institution and work as a composer or music producer, creating soundtracks that move people emotionally.

To my fellow learners: Find something you love, practice with dedication, and share it with the world. Music, like life, is a journey - one note at a time.

# 26

# ANNGAD RAAJ

# Lights, Camera, Action: My Journey as an Actor

## Discovering My Passion for Acting

Hi, I'm Anngad Raaj, and my world comes alive when I step in front of the camera. Ever since I was young, I've been captivated by storytelling - how emotions, expressions, and dialogue come together to create powerful moments on screen. What started as a simple interest in school plays soon turned into a deep passion for acting.

## My First Steps in Acting

My first experience performing in front of an audience was both exciting and nerve-wracking. I still remember standing on stage, feeling the bright lights on my face, and hearing the audience waiting in anticipation. That performance changed everything for me - I realized that acting wasn't just about memorizing lines but about bringing a character to life.

From that moment on, I wanted to explore acting more seriously. I started participating in school dramas, talent competitions, and local theater productions. Each role I played taught me something new about storytelling and human emotions. The thrill of transforming into different characters fueled my passion for performing.

## Overcoming Challenges

Acting isn't always as glamorous as it seems. Memorizing long scripts, mastering body language, and delivering emotions convincingly were challenges I had to work through.

There were times when I struggled with self-doubt, wondering if I was good enough. Facing rejection in auditions was tough, but I learned that every 'no' was just a step closer to a 'yes.'

One of the biggest challenges I faced was balancing my education and acting career. Long rehearsals, multiple takes on set, and traveling for auditions often clashed with my studies. But with the support of 21K School's flexible learning system, I found a way to manage both. My teachers encouraged me to pursue my passion without compromising my education, and that made all the difference.

## Achievements and Milestones

Over the years, I have had the incredible opportunity to work in short films, commercials, and theatrical productions. One of my proudest moments was landing a role in a professional production that allowed me to work alongside experienced actors. The experience of being on set, understanding camera angles, and perfecting my craft was invaluable.

Winning a Best Young Actor award at a local film festival was another milestone that gave me confidence in my abilities. Seeing my hard work recognized reinforced my belief that dedication and perseverance pay off.

## The Role of 21K School

21K School has been instrumental in my journey. The school's innovative approach to learning has allowed me to study at my own pace while pursuing my acting career. Online classes gave me the freedom to attend auditions and shoots without falling behind on my academics. My facilitators and peers have always supported my dreams, motivating me to keep pushing forward.

## Looking Ahead

My ultimate dream is to make a mark in the entertainment industry, not just as an actor but as a storyteller. I want to use my platform to bring meaningful stories to life - stories that inspire, challenge perspectives, and leave a lasting impact on audiences. I plan to continue honing my craft, training with industry professionals, and taking on diverse roles that push my limits as a performer.

To my fellow learners: Dream big, work hard, and never let fear stop you from chasing your passion. Every role you play - whether on stage, on screen, or in life - matters. Make it count.

**27**

# ANUSHREE GURUPRASAD

# Exploring the World Through Reading and Writing

## A Love for Books

Hi, I'm Anushree, a learner who finds joy in books and writing. Reading has always been my escape, taking me to new places, introducing me to new ideas, and inspiring me to write my own stories. From an early age, I was captivated by the way words could build entire worlds, making me feel as though I was traveling through time and space without ever leaving my room.

## Writing My Own Stories

As I read more, I started writing short stories and poems. The more I wrote, the more I discovered my ability to create my own imaginary worlds. Participating in school writing contests helped me refine my skills, and seeing my stories published in a school magazine was one of my proudest moments. Writing gave me confidence - it became my way of expressing my thoughts and emotions, capturing my dreams and ideas on paper.

## Overcoming Writer's Block

Like all writers, I faced moments where words wouldn't come. There were days when I sat staring at a blank page, unsure of how to begin. At first, this was frustrating, but I learned to embrace these moments. Instead of giving up, I would take breaks, read books for inspiration, or simply observe the world around me. My biggest realization was that stories exist everywhere - we just need to listen and capture them.

## Achievements and Recognition

One of my greatest achievements was winning an interschool essay competition. Writing under a time constraint was a challenge, but I learned how to structure my thoughts quickly and effectively. Another proud moment was when my poem about nature was selected for a national-level literary magazine. The joy of seeing my work published motivated me to keep pushing myself creatively.

## The Role of 21K School

21K School has played a crucial role in nurturing my passion for writing. The flexible learning system has given me time to explore my creative side while keeping up with my studies. My facilitators have always encouraged me to participate in literary activities, guiding me on how to improve my storytelling techniques and refine my writing skills. Being in an environment that values creativity has helped me grow immensely as a writer.

## Looking to the Future

My dream is to become an author, creating books that inspire and entertain readers around the world. I want to explore different genres, from fantasy and mystery to poetry and journalism. Writing has taught me patience, creativity, and the power of storytelling. I hope to one day see my books on shelves, touching the hearts of people across the globe.

To my fellow learners: **Read widely, write freely, and let your imagination soar. Every story you write has the power to make a difference. Keep writing, keep dreaming, and never stop creating!**

# 28

## ARYA KOORSE

# Coding My Way to the Future

### Discovering the World of Coding

Hi, I'm Arya Koorse, a learner fascinated by technology and coding. I wrote my first lines of code at the age of 10, and since then, I've been exploring different programming languages and building small projects. Coding felt like unlocking a new superpower - one where I could create anything I imagined, from games to websites and even small automation tools.

### The Thrill of Problem-Solving

Coding is like solving a puzzle. I love breaking down complex problems and finding solutions through logic and creativity. One of my favorite projects was creating a basic game, which made me realize the limitless possibilities of coding. Each challenge I encountered - whether it was a syntax error or a logical bug - taught me patience and resilience. Debugging became a fun challenge rather than a frustrating roadblock.

### Challenges in Learning

Programming can be frustrating, especially when errors keep popping up, and you can't figure out why your code isn't working. There were times I felt like giving up, but I reminded myself that every mistake was an opportunity to learn. I started collaborating with other young coders, learning from online resources, and even taking part in coding competitions to challenge myself further.

## Achievements and Recognition

One of my proudest moments was winning a coding hackathon for learners. I built an interactive quiz app that combined education with entertainment. It was a rewarding experience, not just because of the competition but also because I saw how my creation could be useful for others. Another milestone was getting my first website live, which I developed from scratch using HTML, CSS, and JavaScript.

## The Role of 21K School

21K School played a huge role in helping me nurture my passion for coding. The flexible schedule allowed me to dedicate more time to learning programming while balancing my academics. My facilitators encouraged me to integrate technology into my projects, making learning even more interactive and engaging. The exposure to STEM activities further strengthened my interest in pursuing a career in technology.

## Looking to the Future

I dream of becoming a software engineer and developing innovative solutions that make a difference in people's lives. Whether it's artificial intelligence, app development, or cybersecurity, I want to be at the forefront of technology. My goal is to create tools that help solve real-world problems and make technology accessible to everyone.

To my fellow learners: **Technology is shaping the future. Start learning, stay curious, and keep building!**

**29**

## ASANSHAY

# Kicking Goals, Striking Notes, and Building Dreams

**Exploring My Passions**

Hi, I'm Asanshay, a young and dynamic learner from Mhow, India. My journey is a blend of sports, music, and learning. As a Grade 2MB learner in the British Pathway at 21K School, I've found joy in multiple passions - karate, reading, and playing the keyboard. These pursuits have shaped me into who I am today and have given me a unique perspective on discipline and creativity.

**My Journey in Karate**

Karate has been a transformative experience for me. Winning a gold medal in the Kata event and a silver in the Kumite event at the M.P. State Open Karate Championship in July 2024 was a moment of immense pride. Competing among talented participants and standing on the podium was exhilarating. I still remember the loud cheers and the pride in my parents' eyes - it was a day I'll always cherish. Karate has taught me resilience, discipline, and the importance of perseverance. I now dream of earning a black belt and competing at the national level.

**Music and My Love for the Keyboard**

Apart from karate, my love for music plays a big role in my life. Playing the keyboard brings me joy, and one of my most memorable performances was playing the national anthem on Independence Day at 21K School.

Hours of practice led to that moment, and as I played, I could feel the emotions of my peers and teachers resonate through the music. It wasn't just a performance - it was my way of honoring my country and sharing my love for melodies.

## Overcoming Challenges

Every journey has its challenges, and mine is no different. Karate demands discipline, and one of my biggest struggles has been maintaining a balanced diet. I have a sweet tooth, but I've learned to control my cravings and prioritize a healthy routine to stay fit for training. Another challenge has been staying consistent with karate lessons while traveling. However, my determination pushes me to practice even during trips, using online training sessions to keep up with my learning.

## The Support That Drives Me

Behind every success is a strong support system, and I'm lucky to have my parents as my biggest pillars of strength. They always encourage me to push my limits and pursue my passions fearlessly. My teachers at 21K School have also played a crucial role in my journey. The flexibility of online learning has been a game-changer for me. It saves time, eliminates the stress of commuting, and allows me to focus on what truly matters - learning, growing, and excelling.

## Looking to the Future

With my recent success in the State Championship, I'm now preparing for the National Championship with renewed determination. I hope to continue improving in both karate and music, with the dream of one day writing a book about my experiences.

To my fellow learners: **Believe in yourself and never give up, no matter how tough the path may seem. Every obstacle is an opportunity to grow, and every success begins with a single step.**

# 30

## Avisthita Goyari

# Dancing Through Life: My Journey of Passion

### My Love for Dance

Hi, I'm Avisthita Goyari, a Grade 2 learner from Guwahati, Assam. Dance is not just a hobby for me - it's a passion, a dream, and a way of life. From the moment I took my first steps as a dancer at four years old, I knew that this was what made me happiest. Over the years, I have dedicated myself to perfecting my craft and embracing the beauty of movement.

### Achievements and Big Breaks

In 2024, I was thrilled to win over 70 awards in solo dance competitions. Being part of TV reality shows like Assam Got Talent and Assam Talent Hunt was a dream come true. Performing on such big platforms gave me the confidence to believe in myself. Each performance taught me something new - how to overcome stage fear, how to express emotions through dance, and how to connect with an audience.

### A Day in My Life as a Dancer

My daily routine is filled with energy and movement. I wake up at 6:00 AM to start my dance practice, no matter the weather. By 9:30 AM, I'm ready for school. Some days are even more exciting, especially when I have competitions that go late into the night. I've slept in the car between performances, waking up just in time to go on stage.

My schedule also includes other creative activities. In the afternoons, I enjoy art, tabla, and coding, and in the evenings, I continue learning new dance moves. During festivals like Durga Puja and Bihu, I often perform on multiple stages in a single day. It's challenging, but I've learned to stay focused and organized.

## Overcoming Stage Fear

One of the hardest moments in my journey was when I forgot my steps during a performance. I was so nervous that I froze on stage, feeling tears welling up in my eyes. Some people laughed, and I felt embarrassed. But instead of giving up, I turned to my parents and Guru for guidance. They reminded me that mistakes are part of the journey and that confidence comes with practice. Over time, I built my courage and even improved my public speaking skills.

## The Support That Keeps Me Going

I am incredibly grateful for my parents, who always believe in me and cheer me on every step of the way. My Guru has played a huge role in shaping my skills, teaching me Kathak and acrobatics, which help with flexibility and grace. My facilitators at 21K School, especially Ms. Sheetal Ganatra and Ms. Shweta Basu, have been my biggest supporters in academics. Their encouragement has helped me balance both dance and school effectively.

## Looking to the Future

This journey has taught me that practice, patience, and resilience are key. Some people tell me that I am too young to compete with older dancers, but that only fuels my determination. I dream of representing my country in international dance competitions and inspiring young learners like myself to follow their passion fearlessly.

To my fellow learners: **Never give up. Even slow progress is still progress. Believe in yourself, and you'll achieve your dreams.**

# 31

# Ayaan Thakur C

# The Game That Defines Me

## My First Love: Cricket

Hi, I'm Ayaan, and for as long as I can remember, cricket has been more than just a sport - it has been my passion, my teacher, and my greatest motivator. The first time I picked up a bat at the age of six, I felt an instant connection to the game. The way the ball spun off the bat and soared through the air fascinated me. From that moment, I knew cricket was not just a game I wanted to play, but a journey I wanted to embark on.

## Lessons from the Pitch

Cricket has taught me discipline, perseverance, and teamwork - qualities that go beyond the field and shape my everyday life. Hours of practice, early morning training, and relentless drills have helped me grow both physically and mentally. My parents and coaches have been my pillars of support, pushing me to strive for excellence and improve my skills at every stage.

## A Match to Remember

One of the most unforgettable moments in my cricket journey was the local under-14 championship final. With just a few runs needed and one ball left, I found myself at the crease. The pressure was immense, but I took a deep breath, trusted my training, and swung the bat. As the ball raced to the boundary, the entire team erupted in cheers.

That match was a turning point - it showed me that hard work and self-belief can turn even the toughest situations into victories.

## Facing Setbacks and Bouncing Back

Like any sport, cricket comes with its share of challenges. There were times I missed key shots, dropped catches, or lost games despite giving my best effort. These setbacks were tough, but they taught me resilience. I learned that failure is not the opposite of success but a step toward it. Cricket has also reinforced the importance of teamwork - individual talent means little without the collective effort of the team.

## The Role of 21K School

One of the biggest challenges I faced was balancing my passion for cricket with academics. Thanks to 21K School's flexible learning approach, I was able to manage both. My teachers and facilitators understood my aspirations and supported me in maintaining a balance between school and training. Online learning has allowed me to focus on both my studies and my game without feeling overwhelmed.

## Looking to the Future

I know my journey is just beginning. My goal is to play at the national level, representing my school, my state, and one day, my country. With every match, every practice, and every lesson learned, I move closer to that dream.

To my fellow learners: **Chase your passion relentlessly, embrace the challenges, and trust the process. Hard work and dedication will always lead you to success.**

# 32

# Carmina Fernandes

# Words That Shape My World

## Discovering My Passion for Writing

Hi, I'm Carmina, a Grade 5 learner at 21K School in Mumbai, and I believe that words have the power to change the world. Ever since I could hold a pen, I have loved writing stories, poems, and essays. What started as simple scribbles in a notebook turned into a deep passion for storytelling.

## My Journey as an Author

One of my proudest achievements has been becoming a published author. I have written three books - What Christmas Means to Me, True Love, and My Special Day. The third book was recognized as one of India's Top 100 Bestselling Young Author Books during the Summer Book Writing Festival 2024! Seeing my book displayed at Crossword Stores in Mumbai and featured on Disney International HD was a dream come true.

## Overcoming Challenges

The road to becoming an author hasn't been easy. Balancing my schoolwork and writing was difficult at first, and there were moments when I doubted myself. But I learned the importance of time management. Creating a timetable helped me ensure that I gave equal attention to my academics and writing.

My facilitators at 21K School played a huge role in my success, constantly encouraging me to keep going. My mother, my first mentor, always reminded me that belief in oneself is the key to success.

## The Role of 21K School

Joining 21K School after the COVID-19 pandemic turned out to be one of the best decisions of my life. The school not only gave me the flexibility to pursue my dreams but also introduced me to Lit Fest, Mathalon, and G.K. Quizzes, which helped me expand my knowledge. These activities improved my writing skills and made me more confident in expressing my ideas.

## Finding My Voice

I used to be nervous about public speaking, but my journey as a writer gave me the confidence to express myself. Today, I am proud to host assemblies in my class, engage in discussions, and present my ideas without fear. Writing has helped me become a better communicator and has strengthened my ability to connect with people.

## Looking to the Future

My dream is to write books that inspire and uplift others. I want my stories to spark imagination, instill confidence, and spread positivity. With the support of 21K School and platforms like BriBooks, I know I can continue to grow as a writer. There is still so much I want to learn and achieve, and I am excited for what the future holds.

To all learners: **Never let anyone tell you that you cannot achieve something. Stay positive, work hard, and follow your passion. Success is not about never failing - it's about rising every time you fall.**

I am excited to see what's next in my journey, and I hope to inspire others to find their voice, just as I have found mine.

# 33

# DHANASVI SHARMA

# Rising Strong: A Journey of Grit and Glory

## A Fighter's Spirit

Hi, I'm Dhanasvi Sharma, and my journey has been a testament to resilience, determination, and hard work. My life revolves around two major passions - academics and Pencak Silat, a martial art that has shaped my mind and body. From the moment I stepped onto the training mat, I knew this sport was more than just physical strength; it required focus, discipline, and an unbreakable spirit.

## Triumph on the World Stage

My passion for Pencak Silat has taken me to places I never imagined. Winning two consecutive gold medals at the National Pencak Silat Championships was a milestone, but my proudest moment was representing India at the World Championship and bringing home a gold medal. Standing on that podium, with the Indian flag waving behind me, I felt an overwhelming sense of pride - not just for myself, but for my family, my mentors, and everyone who believed in me.

## Overcoming Life's Toughest Battles

Behind these achievements lies a story of perseverance. Balancing intense sports training with my academics was never easy. My days started early and ended late, often leaving little time for anything else. Just when I thought I had found my rhythm, life threw a curveball - my mother needed a kidney transplant. It was a difficult time emotionally and financially for my family.

Watching her endure so much pain was heartbreaking, but it also taught me the true meaning of resilience. I knew I had to stay strong - not just for myself, but for my family.

## The Role of 21K School in My Success

During those tough times, I realized that no journey is ever walked alone. My family became my rock, providing endless support even as they juggled their struggles. 21K School stepped in at the right time, making sure I had the flexibility to keep up with both my training and academics. The personalized learning schedules helped me stay on track, while the constant encouragement from my teachers kept me motivated. Their mentorship and financial sponsorship lightened my family's burden and allowed me to focus on my goals.

## Lessons Learned and the Road Ahead

Through it all, I clung to the belief that challenges are just opportunities in disguise. I developed a disciplined routine, practiced mental resilience, and found strength in small victories. Every late-night study session, every exhausting practice, and every moment of doubt became stepping stones to my success.

Looking ahead, I dream of representing India at the Olympics and pursuing a career in sports management. My journey has taught me that success isn't just about medals or accolades - it's about the courage to keep going when the odds are against you.

To anyone facing challenges, I say this: **"Success is not final, failure is not fatal - it is the courage to continue that counts."**

34

## DHRUV MANDHANE

# Strength in Verses: My Journey with the Bhagavad Gita

## A Unique Passion

Hi, I'm Dhruv Mandhane, a dedicated learner from Mumbai in 21K School's Indian Pathway. While I love outdoor activities like squash, skating, and cycling, one of my proudest achievements has been reciting the 5th Adhyay of the Bhagavad Gita. This experience was more than just a competition - it was a journey of dedication, perseverance, and self-discovery.

## The Challenge of Learning Sanskrit Verses

The Bhagavad Gita is written in Sanskrit, a language rich in meaning but challenging to master. Memorizing the complex pronunciations and understanding the philosophical depth of each verse required patience and effort. At times, I struggled to grasp the meanings and rhythms, but I knew that if I took small steps, I could reach my goal.

## How I Overcame the Challenge

I adopted a structured approach to learning. Instead of trying to memorize everything at once, I broke the task into smaller steps. I started with simpler verses and gradually moved on to the more complex ones. My guru, Lalitha Ma'am, played a crucial role in simplifying the teachings for me. She made learning fun by incorporating storytelling, games, and songs. These interactive methods helped me engage deeply with the verses and retain them more effectively.

## The Role of 21K School in My Success

21K School's innovative approach to learning was instrumental in my journey. The Habits of Mind framework helped me stay focused and persistent. Habits like striving for accuracy, thinking flexibly, and communicating with clarity guided me through the process. With the school's encouragement, I performed confidently during the competition and earned a medal for my achievement.

## Lessons Beyond the Competition

Reciting the Bhagavad Gita wasn't just about winning a medal. The verses instilled valuable life lessons in me - gratitude, honesty, respect, and self-discipline. I learned that success isn't about chasing rewards but about the dedication and sincerity we put into our work. These teachings have shaped me into a more focused and reflective learner.

## Looking to the Future

This experience has strengthened my memory, critical thinking, and problem-solving skills - abilities that will guide me in all areas of life. My next goal is to continue learning Sanskrit and explore more chapters of the Bhagavad Gita. I also hope to inspire other young learners to take on challenges fearlessly.

To anyone working towards a difficult goal, my advice is simple: **"Never give up. Through constant practice and perseverance, you can achieve great things."**

I am deeply grateful to my family, my guru, my friends, and my school for their unwavering support. Their belief in me made this achievement possible. The message from the Bhagavad Gita, **"Do your duty, but do not be attached to the results,"** continues to inspire me. I hope it inspires you too!

# 35

# Dhruvika P

# A Path Reimagined: From Science to Law

## Finding My True Calling

Hi, I'm Dhruvika P, and my journey has been a story of transformation, resilience, and passion. For most of my school years, I was immersed in science. I enjoyed the logical approach of scientific thinking, and for a long time, I believed that my future lay in that direction. However, deep down, I had an interest that refused to fade - law. The thought of advocating for justice, standing up for people, and debating complex ideas intrigued me. But moving from a science background to law seemed like an impossible shift.

## The Struggles of Transition

Switching fields is never easy, and I faced my fair share of challenges. The idea of transitioning to arts and law felt daunting. The fear of leaving behind everything I had studied and stepping into an entirely new academic world was overwhelming. However, after deep reflection, I realized that my true passion lay in understanding justice, social change, and governance rather than scientific theories.

This realization came towards the end of Class 11, when I started exploring my interests beyond textbooks. Literature, arts, and legal studies began to excite me more than equations and lab experiments. But the journey of transition wasn't just about academic shifts - it also meant preparing myself emotionally and mentally for a completely new learning experience.

## The Role of 21K School

One of the biggest turning points was joining 21K School's NIOS program. The flexibility of online schooling allowed me to manage both my academics and my preparations for law school. The transition wasn't immediate - it took time to adjust to different subjects, understand legal concepts, and change my study approach. But with the support of my teachers, I developed a structured plan that kept me on track.

21K School didn't just provide academic support - it introduced me to MUNs (Model United Nations), guest lectures, and workshops that broadened my perspective on global issues. These experiences made me realize that law was not just about rules - it was about understanding people, cultures, and justice.

## The Road to Law School

Preparing for CLAT (Common Law Admission Test) was one of the toughest phases of my journey. The competition was intense, and self-doubt often crept in. I had moments where I questioned whether I had made the right decision. But with the help of my mentor Manav Lawania, who guided me through mock tests, legal reasoning, and strategies, I began to see progress. My family and friends also played an important role in keeping me motivated.

## Achievements and Lessons Learned

All the challenges and hard work finally paid off when I got admitted into NLSIU Bangalore - one of India's top law schools. Along the way, I also achieved several milestones, including winning the IEO Gold Medal, securing a national-level rank (8th), and serving as the Vice President of Studomatrix, a learner-led organization. These experiences strengthened my ability to lead, communicate, and stay committed to my goals.

## Looking Ahead

My goal is not just to build a career in law but to contribute to meaningful social change. I want to explore the impact of law on marginalized communities, advocate for policy reforms, and make a difference in the justice system. My journey has taught me that passion is more important than convention - it's never too late to change paths and follow what truly excites you.

To my fellow learners: **Trust your instincts, don't be afraid to pivot, and always believe that the right path will reveal itself with time and dedication.**

# 36

# DR. SWAYAM SODHA

# The Making of a Young Technopreneur

## A Passion for Innovation

Hi, I'm Dr. Swayam Sodha, a 10-year-old learner from Mumbai, Bharat. My journey so far has been filled with curiosity, passion, and a relentless drive to innovate. From a young age, I was fascinated by technology, gadgets, and coding. What started as an interest soon turned into a deep passion, pushing me to explore fields like data science, machine learning, and artificial intelligence.

## Achievements in Technology

One of my biggest milestones was earning a Doctorate in Information Technology, making me one of India's youngest technopreneurs. My dream has always been to build technology that makes life better, and this dream led me to found my own company - Swayamezon Smart-Wear Technologies, where I work on futuristic products integrating IoT, AI, AR, XR, and edge computing.

## The Challenge of Balancing Innovation and Learning

Managing school, coding, research, and business projects is no easy task. There were times when my schedule felt overwhelming, especially while traveling for awards and presentations. But 21K School's flexible online learning model allowed me to keep up with my academics while pursuing my passion. The school also arranged one-on-one Sanskrit classes and ensured that I had the technical resources to keep learning without disruptions.

## Recognition and Awards

My work in technology has led me to some incredible recognitions, including:

- Pride of Bharat Award (Government of India)
- Radiant Rising Star Award (Chennai)
- Meeting investor Ronnie Screwvala at UpGrad, who inspired me to dream even bigger

These moments reinforced my belief that age is never a barrier to achieving big things.

## Lessons from My Journey

My journey as a technopreneur has taught me that success is about more than just skills - it's about resilience, time management, and having the right mindset. Every project, whether successful or not, has been an opportunity to learn, improve, and innovate.

I believe that the future of technology is about solving real-world problems. My next goal is to develop smart wearables that enhance healthcare and daily living. Technology should not only be advanced but also accessible and impactful.

## Words for Future Innovators

To my fellow learners: Be like the 3 Idiots - ask questions, stay curious, and never stop learning. Your age does not define your ability to create something great. Discover your strengths, nurture them, and chase your dreams fearlessly.

I want to thank my parents for their unwavering support, my teachers for their guidance, and YouTube for being my constant learning companion.

As I continue this journey, I remind myself every day: **"Weave your will; go get your goal!"**

# 37

# EEDYAAY PATTANAYAK

# From Maps to Milestones: A Journey of Discovery

## The Explorer's Spirit

Hi, I'm Eedyaay Pattanayak, a learner of KG-2MB at 21K School in Gurugram, India. My journey is filled with curiosity, adventure, and learning. Whether it's exploring maps, aviation, skating, or music, I embrace every opportunity to discover and grow. My love for new experiences has taught me resilience, creativity, and the importance of lifelong learning.

## A Passion for Maps and Aviation

My fascination with maps and geography defines me as a cartophile. I spend hours on Google Maps and Google Earth, discovering new places, tracing routes, and understanding different terrains. My passion for aviation keeps me engaged in plane-spotting, flight simulations, and learning about airlines and airports. The thrill of watching a plane take off and land never fails to excite me. I dream of becoming a pilot one day, soaring through the skies and exploring the world from above.

## The World of Sports and Music

Beyond maps and aviation, I am deeply invested in sports and music. Skating keeps me active, focused, and energetic, while playing the keyboard brings rhythm and creativity into my life. One of my proudest achievements was securing 3rd place in the District-Level Roll Ball U-9 Championship and another 3rd place in an inter-school skating competition.

These experiences have taught me the values of dedication, discipline, and sportsmanship.

## Overcoming Challenges

My journey has not been without challenges. Moving from the UK to India at the age of four was a major transition. Adapting to a new country, language, and climate took time. One of the toughest adjustments was learning Hindi, as my skating coach primarily spoke the language. At first, I struggled to communicate, but with effort and practice, I overcame the language barrier. Adjusting to India's warm and humid climate after growing up in the cooler UK weather was another hurdle. Despite these challenges, I persevered with determination and embraced my new environment.

## The Role of 21K School

21K School has played a vital role in my growth. My teachers celebrated my achievements in skating and music, boosting my confidence. The school's flexible online classes allowed me to balance my academics and hobbies seamlessly. Engaging in creative activities, such as making self-portraits, helped me bond with classmates and express my individuality. The British curriculum nurtured my imagination, empowering me to publish my first book, Blackways and His Adventures - an achievement that makes me incredibly proud.

## Looking to the Future

This journey has taught me essential life lessons in adaptability, communication, and perseverance. I've learned to embrace change, understand the power of mutual respect, and grow stronger through challenges. Looking ahead, I aspire to explore my passions further, set new goals, and push my boundaries.

To my fellow learners: **Embrace your uniqueness and pursue your dreams without limits.**

# 38

## ESPERANCE SOARES

# Navigating the Hustle: A Story of Growth and Grit

### Becoming a Young Entrepreneur

Hi, I'm Esperance Soares, a Grade 8 learner at 21K School, and my journey is one of resilience, ambition, and determination. At just 14 years old, I am not only managing my academics but also running a thriving business that fulfills over 600 orders weekly. Entrepreneurship wasn't something I planned - it just happened. What started as a simple idea quickly transformed into an exciting venture filled with challenges and growth.

### The Balancing Act: School and Business

Managing a business at my age means juggling multiple responsibilities. Some days feel impossibly long, with workshops, customer orders, and assignments demanding my attention. Traveling for business events often means I have less time to study, but I have learned to adapt and prioritize effectively. The most important lesson I have learned is that success isn't about having everything under control - it's about learning to adapt and keep moving forward.

### Overcoming Setbacks and Staying Motivated

Like any entrepreneur, I've faced setbacks. There were moments when orders piled up, customers had issues, and deadlines seemed impossible to meet. I had to learn patience, time management, and the ability to stay calm under pressure.

My family and mentors have been my strongest support system, always encouraging me to push forward even when things got tough.

## The Role of 21K School

21K School has been a game-changer for me. Their flexible online learning model has allowed me to manage both school and business seamlessly. Recorded lessons let me catch up on classes at my own pace, even when I'm traveling. There were times when I took exams in airports or between business meetings, and the unwavering support from my teachers made it possible. Knowing that my facilitators believe in me has been a major source of motivation.

## Lessons in Leadership and Growth

This journey has transformed me in ways I never imagined. I've learned to manage my time efficiently, stay focused on my goals, and embrace challenges as opportunities to grow. My experiences have taught me that resilience isn't just about pushing through difficulties - it's about learning from them and evolving.

## Hobbies That Keep Me Grounded

Beyond business, I have hobbies that keep me balanced and energized. Swimming and cycling help me stay active and clear my mind, while music fuels my creativity. These activities allow me to recharge and maintain focus amidst my demanding schedule.

## Looking to the Future

I aspire to scale my business even further while continuing my academic journey. I want to inspire others - especially young learners like me - to dream big and work hard to turn those dreams into reality. My message to anyone reading this is simple: **never give up on your vision, no matter how steep the climb or how long the journey. Success may not come immediately, but with patience and persistence, it will eventually find its way to you.**

**39**

## GEET

# Beyond the Stars: A Journey of Curiosity and Change

### A Dream Written in the Stars

Hi, I'm Geet, a Grade 10 learner, and my journey began with a simple dream: to explore the stars. As a child, I would gaze at the night sky, wondering about the mysteries beyond. My love for space was more than just fascination - it was a calling. This passion led me to Space Camp, an experience that changed the course of my life and solidified my purpose.

### A Defining Experience at Space Camp

At Space Camp, I didn't just learn about rockets and space missions - I learned the power of teamwork, problem-solving, and global collaboration. Surrounded by brilliant young minds from around the world, I realized that space exploration was not just about astronauts and engineers; it required a collective effort from diverse fields. This realization broadened my perspective, igniting a desire to make a real impact on the world.

### Writing for Change

My passion for space evolved into something even greater - writing and advocacy. I began participating in international essay competitions, including the John Locke Institute Global Essay Prize and the International Christian University Global Youth Essay Competition. Writing about democracy, human rights, and global challenges helped me understand the power of words in shaping ideas and inspiring change.

Winning recognition on international platforms was not just an honor - it was validation that my voice mattered.

## A Scholarship That Opened New Doors

One of my proudest achievements was receiving a scholarship to study Philosophy, Politics, and Economics (PPE) in Singapore. This program combined my love for critical thinking, governance, and problem-solving, giving me an opportunity to deepen my understanding of the world. It was a reminder that persistence and passion could create life-changing opportunities.

## Breaking Barriers with She Shakti

Being a young woman in STEM came with its challenges. Society often set limits on what I could achieve, but the She Shakti leadership program empowered me to break barriers, challenge norms, and embrace my potential. It reminded me that resilience and self-belief could turn obstacles into stepping stones.

## Recognition and Inspiration

My journey gained recognition when platforms like India Today and The Better India featured my story. Seeing my experiences inspire others - especially young girls - was one of the most rewarding moments of my life. Meeting entrepreneur Ronnie Screwvala further strengthened my resolve to think beyond personal success and strive to make a meaningful impact on society.

## The Role of 21K School

21K School has been a pillar of support, allowing me to balance academics with my ambitions. The flexible learning environment and encouragement from my teachers helped me realize that dreams are attainable with the right mindset and perseverance.

### Looking Ahead

My journey - from Space Camp to global recognition - is just the beginning. My dream is to contribute to scientific research, policymaking, and advocacy to create a better future for the next generation. If my story can inspire just one person to chase their dreams, then I know I've made a difference.

To my fellow learners: **The stars are within reach for those who believe. Dream big, work hard, and never stop reaching for the impossible.**

# 40

## HAMZAH MALIK

# The Strategic Mind: My Journey Through Chess

### A Game of Endless Possibilities

Hi, I'm Hamzah Malik, a Grade 4 learner at 21K School from Srinagar, India. Chess is more than just a game to me - it's a passion, a challenge, and a way of life. Every move I make on the board teaches me about strategy, patience, and perseverance. My journey in chess has been one of growth, setbacks, and unwavering determination.

### Competing on the International Stage

One of my biggest achievements came in January 2024 when I participated in the 2nd Matrix Cup International Open FIDE Rating Chess Tournament in New Delhi. Competing against 595 participants was an intimidating yet thrilling experience. Moving from state-level to national-level competitions was a significant step forward and boosted my confidence tremendously.

### Winning at Different Levels

This year, I secured first place in UT-level tournaments across multiple categories - Under-09, Under-13, Under-15, and Under-19. In June 2024, I finished as runner-up in the Under-17 category. Every match I played taught me something new and motivated me to improve my game further.

## Overcoming Challenges

Being in Srinagar, I don't have many opportunities to participate in offline tournaments. Most of my training happens online, which isn't the same as facing an opponent across the board. Losing a game can be frustrating, but I've learned to see every loss as a lesson. I stay motivated by studying grandmasters' games, solving puzzles, and continuously refining my tactics.

## The Role of Family and School

My family has been my biggest support system. My father travels with me to tournaments, ensuring I get exposure to top-level competition, while my mother helps me manage schoolwork when I'm busy with chess. At 21K School, the flexibility of recorded classes allows me to catch up on lessons after tournaments, making it easier to balance academics and chess.

## The Lessons Chess Has Taught Me

Chess has given me invaluable life lessons - how to make thoughtful decisions, stay calm under pressure, and bounce back from failure. Losing a game no longer discourages me; instead, it drives me to analyze my mistakes and come back stronger.

## Looking to the Future

My dream is to become a Chess Grandmaster and represent India on the global stage. I train 3 to 4 hours daily with my coach and keep competing to sharpen my skills. Whenever I feel like giving up, I remind myself of my motto: **"Perseverance is the key to success. Work hard, and never lose hope."**

To my fellow learners: **Keep trying, keep believing, and never let setbacks define you. The game of life - just like chess - is all about making the right moves at the right time.**

# 41

# HANU MIRDULA

# The Art of Strength and Grace

## A Dual Passion

Hi, I'm Hanu Mirdula, a dedicated learner from 21K British School in Chennai, India. My life is deeply intertwined with two powerful traditions of my culture - Bharatanatyam and Silambam. These two disciplines, though seemingly different, have shaped me into a more confident, focused, and disciplined individual.

## A Journey Through Bharatanatyam

Bharatanatyam has been a part of my life for as long as I can remember. The graceful movements, intricate footwork, and expressive storytelling make it more than just a dance - it's an art form that connects me to my heritage. Through years of practice, I have learned discipline, patience, and perseverance, traits that have helped me in every other aspect of my life. Performing on stage gives me an unmatched sense of joy and fulfillment.

## Mastering Silambam: The Martial Art of Precision

Alongside Bharatanatyam, I have developed a strong passion for Silambam, an ancient Indian martial art that demands precision, agility, and mental strength. Competing in state-level championships was one of the most challenging yet rewarding experiences of my journey. When I secured second place in my first competition, I was both proud and motivated to push harder. I trained rigorously, refining my skills and techniques, and eventually, I won first place at the state level.

## Overcoming Challenges

Balancing rigorous Silambam training, Bharatanatyam rehearsals, and academics was not easy. There were times when exhaustion took over, and I felt overwhelmed. However, I learned the art of time management and resilience. Creating a structured routine helped me prioritize both my studies and my practice sessions. Staying calm under pressure was another skill I developed, which significantly improved my performance in both competitions and academics.

## The Role of 21K School

21K School played a crucial role in my journey. The flexibility of online learning allowed me to dedicate time to my passions while keeping up with my studies. My teachers provided constant support, encouraging me to chase my dreams while excelling academically. Resources like ATL and HOM helped enhance my problem-solving and critical-thinking skills, which proved useful in both my art forms.

## Looking Ahead

This journey has taught me that success is a result of hard work, perseverance, and a strong support system. I aspire to continue excelling in both Bharatanatyam and Silambam, pushing my limits while inspiring others to embrace their passions fearlessly.

To my fellow learners: Your journey is your own. Never give up, stay determined, and always believe in yourself. Every challenge you overcome makes you stronger.

# 42

# Hareharr Bharuka

## Juggling Passion, Academics, and Dreams

### A Dream Beyond the Ordinary

Hi, I'm Hareharr Bharuka, a learner pursuing A Levels under the British Curriculum in Aurangabad, Maharashtra. While academics are important, my heart belongs to my three biggest passions - cooking, football, and gaming. My journey has been about balancing these interests while achieving academic and personal milestones.

### Research and Recognition

One of my proudest achievements was collaborating with Boston University on a research project. Being selected for this opportunity was an incredible honor, and it allowed me to contribute meaningful work to both my school and a prestigious institution. Another highlight of my journey was being selected for an exclusive event at my college, where only 15 out of 200 learners were chosen. These experiences reaffirmed that I am on the right path.

### The Challenge of Time Management

One of the biggest challenges I faced was time management. Pursuing multiple passions meant balancing academics, sports, and culinary arts, all while meeting deadlines and keeping up with responsibilities. Some nights, I would return home past midnight after football practice, only to wake up early for school the next day. Rather than letting exhaustion overwhelm me, I learned to make time my ally.

By structuring my day efficiently, I found a way to dedicate time to my interests without sacrificing my academic performance. 21K School's guidance and the flexibility of online learning played a significant role in helping me maintain this balance.

## Football and Gaming: More Than Just Hobbies

Football has always been a major part of my life. The sport has taught me teamwork, discipline, and leadership skills that extend beyond the field. Gaming, on the other hand, is not just a pastime but an arena where I develop strategic thinking and decision-making skills. I believe that every interest, no matter how unconventional, contributes to personal growth in unexpected ways.

## The Role of 21K School

21K School has played a transformational role in shaping my academic and personal journey. My business teacher, Sonali Ma'am, introduced me to time management techniques, which have helped me immensely. The school also provided opportunities to participate in events like Literary Fest and cultural celebrations, which helped me build confidence and create lasting memories.

## Looking to the Future

Despite my varied interests, my ultimate dream remains the same as it was five years ago - to become a renowned chef. Many people may find this dream unconventional, but I believe in myself more than anything else. With hard work, determination, and an unwavering belief in my abilities, I know I will make my dream a reality.

To my fellow learners: **Chase your dreams with passion and perseverance. Don't let anyone tell you what's impossible - because with belief in yourself, anything is possible.**

As I continue on this path, I am grateful to my family, teachers, and peers who have supported me every step of the way. The best is yet to come!

**43**

# HRRIDAY YESHWANTH RAJ

# Blending Creativity, Leadership, and Passion

## A Journey of Exploration

Hi, I'm Hrriday Yeshwanth Raj, an 8-year-old learner from Raipur, India, studying in the British Pathway of 21K School for the last 5 years. I have always been inquisitive about science and math to art, from creative problem solving to working on sports, from authoring books to nurturing business ideas.I find joy in creating, learning, and pushing boundaries.

## Sold my painting when I was five

What started as simple doodles with crayons has now turned into paintings displayed in homes across India and abroad. I have sold quite a few paintings and gifted many. One of my proudest moments was showcasing my work at the largest art exhibition in Central India. I sold my first painting when I was five and have continued to explore my artistic side.

## Becoming an Author at Seven

I authored and illustrated my first book, The Magical Peapod, when I was seven. I was recognised as the 19th Best Selling Author at the National Young Authors Fair, India. My book was showcased at the prestigious Brooklyn Book Festival in New York and is available on Amazon with an ISBN allocated and a copyright registered in my name.

## Football and Entrepreneurship

Football is my third love. Whether it's watching matches, analysing plays, or competing on the field, the game energises me. But I wanted to take my love for football beyond just playing. That's when I came up with the idea of organising a 'Kids vs Adults' football league. This helped me to learn the nuances of branding and marketing to managing operations and teams, I learned the fundamentals of business, leadership and teamwork. I'm not just playing or simply enjoying these activities; I'm actively engaging in them with a business-minded approach.

## Overcoming Challenges

My journey has not been without its hurdles. Losing football matches, facing rejection for my artwork, or hitting writer's block while working on my stories have often made me question my abilities. But each challenge has taught me to stay resilient, break down problems into smaller steps, and never stop believing in myself.

## The Role of 21K School

The flexibility of 21K School's online format has played a huge role in my ability to balance my interests. The project-based learning approach has helped me develop critical thinking and problem-solving skills, which I apply in everything I do. The encouragement from my facilitators has been invaluable, motivating me to pursue my dreams fearlessly.

## Looking to the Future

I envision myself as an entrepreneur, innovator, and changemaker, solving real-world problems through creativity and passion. I know my journey will be one of exploration and impact. I truly believe in the words of APJ Abdul Kalam, "If you want to shine like a sun, first burn like a sun." To my fellow learners: **Don't think about the world; just play the game of your life.**

# 44

## Innaam Faizal

# The Balancing Act: Passion, Learning, and Leadership

### Exploring a World of Interests

Hi, I'm Innaam Faizal, and my journey is all about balancing my love for programming, mathematics, teaching, and leadership. From an early age, I was captivated by solving problems and exploring new ideas. Whether it was coding, participating in Model United Nations (MUN), or teaching others, I found fulfillment in everything I did.

### Leading the Way in Space Innovation

One of the most exciting moments in my life was leading my team at NASA SpaceApps 2022, where we won the Local People's Choice Award. This competition was more than just a test of technical skills - it was about collaboration, teamwork, and innovation. Solving space-related challenges with like-minded individuals gave me a deeper appreciation for science, research, and global problem-solving.

### Teaching for a Cause

Beyond technology, I have always believed in giving back to the community. Working with Teach For Speech (TFS) Bangalore Chapter, I advocated for education among underprivileged children, helping them build their confidence in public speaking and communication. Teaching others reinforced my own understanding of subjects and improved my leadership abilities.

## Overcoming Challenges

Balancing academics, extracurriculars, and personal projects was never easy. There were times when exam seasons clashed with major competitions, making it difficult to manage everything. I often wondered if I could excel in every area I cared about. Through these struggles, I learned valuable lessons in time management, prioritization, and self-awareness. Instead of comparing grades or achievements with others, I focused on improving my study habits and using online resources like SaveMyExams and Cognito. Structured study plans and better organization helped me boost my academic performance and self-confidence.

## The Role of 21K School

21K School transformed my learning experience. Their personalized lesson plans and creative approach allowed me to thrive in multiple areas. Initially, I was hesitant to join MUN, but once I did, I discovered a newfound passion for debate, diplomacy, and public speaking. Anchoring school events in 9th and 10th grade sharpened my communication skills, and the school's emphasis on innovation and critical thinking helped me grow in ways I never imagined.

## Looking to the Future

Through this journey, I've realized that setbacks don't define us - our response to them does. Leadership, which once felt intimidating, is now something I embrace. Time management, which was once a struggle, is now my strength. My goal is to become a professor and contribute to global education, creating opportunities for learners from all backgrounds.

To my fellow learners: **A comeback is always possible if you're willing to work hard and adapt. Stay curious, stay persistent, and the world will open doors for you.**

# 45

# Ivaan Mathur

# A Journey of Curiosity and Achievement

## Embracing Learning and Exploration

Hi, I'm Ivaan Mathur, a KG2 learner at 21K School in Gurugram, India. My journey has been filled with discoveries, achievements, and moments of perseverance. I have always been fascinated by books, Lego, art, and creative thinking, and my love for learning has shaped my experiences both inside and outside the classroom.

## Running the Distance: My Marathon Experience

One of my proudest achievements was participating in my first marathon, the Kanyathon, in Gurugram. Running alongside older participants was both exciting and challenging, but I didn't give up. The thrill of crossing the finish line filled me with a sense of pride. A few months later, I pushed myself further by completing a 3-kilometer marathon in May 2024. These experiences taught me the value of determination and discipline. Every step I took reminded me that perseverance is the key to achieving anything.

## A Passion for Reading and Storytelling

Books have always been a source of inspiration for me. I participated in the British Council's Reading Challenge in New Delhi, where I was required to read four books in four weeks. But my love for stories took over, and I ended up reading 13 books and submitting reviews for all of them! This experience not only strengthened my reading skills but also helped me express my thoughts better through writing.

Being felicitated by Mr. Michael Houlgate, Deputy Director of the British Council, was a proud moment that reinforced my love for books and storytelling.

## Achievements in Sports and Beyond

My journey has been about more than just books and marathons. I took part in the annual sports event organized by 21K School in Delhi, where I competed in various athletic activities. Winning Gold, Silver, and Bronze medals was a rewarding experience, teaching me the spirit of sportsmanship and healthy competition. These experiences have helped me develop confidence, resilience, and teamwork skills.

## The Role of 21K School in My Growth

Balancing academics with all my activities wasn't always easy, but 21K School's flexible online learning system played a crucial role in making it possible. The personalized learning plans helped me stay on track while allowing me to explore my interests. The school's Show-and-Tell activities helped me build my confidence in public speaking and presentation skills, making me a better communicator and team player.

## Looking to the Future

Reflecting on my journey, I realize how much I have grown - not just in academics, but as a person. The lessons I've learned about hard work, determination, and curiosity will always stay with me. As I continue to explore new challenges and set higher goals, I am excited about the future and all the opportunities ahead.

To my fellow learners: **Believe in yourself, explore new possibilities, and never stop learning. Every step forward brings you closer to your dreams.**

# 46

## JAIDITYA SETH

# Aiming for Greatness: My Journey in Tennis and Music

## The Sport That Drives Me

Hi, I'm Jaiditya Seth, a learner at Indian School, Gurugram, and for me, tennis is more than just a game - it's a way of life. Every time I step onto the court, I feel focused, energized, and determined. The journey has been filled with victories, challenges, and moments of self-discovery, shaping me into the player and person I am today.

## Achievements on the Court

Competing at the national level has been one of the most defining experiences of my life. Some of my biggest milestones include:

- Runner-up at the All India U-14 Tennis Tournament (Amritsar) – A moment that proved to me that I could compete with the best.

- Doubles Champion in an All India U-14 Tournament – This victory highlighted the power of teamwork and strategy.

- Consistently reaching four semi-finals and three quarter-finals in major tournaments – These experiences helped me build resilience, mental strength, and self-belief.

## Music and Martial Arts: My Parallel Passions

Beyond tennis, I have a deep passion for music and martial arts. I have been learning the tabla for the past three years, recently completing my 3rd-year exam and preparing for the 4th year. Music brings balance to my life, helping me develop rhythm, focus, and patience. Additionally, earning my green and blue belts in taekwondo has strengthened my physical endurance and mental discipline.

## Overcoming Challenges

My journey hasn't been without struggles. Facing high-ranked opponents in matches tested my confidence, but I learned that success comes from trusting my preparation and improving with each game. Mental resilience became just as important as physical strength. There were times when balancing tennis, academics, and music felt overwhelming, but through discipline and time management, I found a way to excel in all areas.

## The Role of 21K School

Joining 21K School was a game-changer for me. Its flexible class schedules, recorded lessons, and personalized guidance allowed me to dedicate myself to tennis without compromising my academics. Programs like Habits of Mind (HOM) and ATL helped me develop creativity, problem-solving, and adaptability - skills that extend beyond the classroom.

## Looking to the Future

My ultimate dream is to make history as the first Indian to win a Grand Slam title. In the short term, I aim to break into the top 20 national rankings and reach the quarter-finals of an ITF tournament. I know that every challenge I overcome brings me one step closer to my goals.

## Words of Encouragement

If there's one thing I've learned, it's that persistence is key. Every setback, every loss, and every challenge is a chance to grow, adapt, and come back stronger.

To my fellow learners: **Challenges are stepping stones to greatness. Believe in yourself, stay disciplined, and never stop striving for your dreams.**

# 47

## Jitspeed

# The Champion's Mind: A Story of Perseverance and Creativity

### A Passion for Storytelling and Writing

Hi, I'm Jitspeed, and my journey is a blend of writing, martial arts, and public speaking. I have always believed that words have the power to shape ideas and change the world. My literary journey began with The Legend of Icarus - Flight of Destiny, a novel that combined my love for storytelling with mathematical and scientific elements. Its sequel, The Legend of Icarus - The New Generation, expanded this imaginative world, showcasing my evolving creativity.

### Writing for a Purpose

One of my proudest achievements was publishing a national bestseller, The Tattling Sound in the Bush, through BriBooks. This book takes readers on an exciting journey, unraveling insights about the body, mind, and soul in an engaging way. My latest work, The Big Backyard Bush, celebrates friendship and imagination, using the backdrop of cricket to tell a powerful story. Writing has not only given me a voice but also a platform to inspire others.

### Martial Arts and the Spirit of Discipline

Beyond writing, I have always been drawn to karate. Competing in major tournaments has shaped my resilience and character. At the 10th Kicks & Punches Cup in Chennai (2023), I won two gold medals in the Boys' Advanced Kata and Mixed Kata categories. Later, at the 11th Ooty National Karate Championship, I secured a silver medal, proving to myself that hard work and perseverance always pay off.

## Embracing Public Speaking

Public speaking has been another major milestone in my journey. Through the Youth Leadership Program of the Athena International Toastmasters Club, I developed the confidence to speak in front of audiences. The biggest breakthrough came when I became the youngest Indian to deliver a TEDx talk at TEDxBVBRaipur. Sharing my journey - from my dreams to my accomplishments - was a defining moment that reinforced my belief in the power of communication.

## Giving Back Through Philanthropy

One of my most fulfilling decisions was donating all proceeds from my book sales to the TANKER Foundation, an NGO dedicated to supporting those in need. This experience showed me that creativity can serve a greater purpose, and that success is most meaningful when it helps others.

## The Role of 21K School

21K School has provided the flexibility and support I needed to balance my academics with my passions. The school's self-paced learning approach allowed me to dedicate time to my books, karate, and public speaking without compromising my studies. The encouragement from my facilitators gave me the confidence to push boundaries and dream big.

## Looking to the Future

As I continue to grow, I want to inspire others to pursue their passions fearlessly. Whether through writing, martial arts, or public speaking, my journey is a testament to perseverance, creativity, and kindness.

To my fellow learners: **Embrace challenges, think beyond limits, and always stay true to yourself. The world needs your unique voice and talents.**

# 48

# KABIR PAREKH

# The Making of a Tennis Champion

## A Love for Tennis

Hi, I'm Kabir Parekh, an 11-year-old tennis player, and my journey with tennis started at just three years old. Inspired by my father, who is an excellent tennis player, I picked up a racket and never looked back. Tennis is not just a sport to me - it's a passion, a challenge, and a way of life.

## Rising Through the Ranks

At nine years old, I won my first state championship in Kolkata, West Bengal, becoming Bengal's No. 1 player in the Under-10 category. The following year, I made history by winning the state championship again, becoming the only player to win back-to-back titles in this category. After proving myself at the state level, I moved on to national tournaments.

In Lucknow, at an All India Tennis Association (AITA) tournament, I achieved one of my biggest milestones: winning both singles and doubles titles, earning a double crown. This victory reinforced my confidence and fueled my ambition to compete internationally.

## The Spain Experience: Taking Tennis to the Next Level

Recognizing my potential, my parents made a bold decision - they sent me to Barcelona, Spain, for three months of intensive tennis training. Competing in Spain was a completely new experience, as I faced strong international players in the Monty Tour Under-14 category.

## Embracing Public Speaking

Public speaking has been another major milestone in my journey. Through the Youth Leadership Program of the Athena International Toastmasters Club, I developed the confidence to speak in front of audiences. The biggest breakthrough came when I became the youngest Indian to deliver a TEDx talk at TEDxBVBRaipur. Sharing my journey - from my dreams to my accomplishments - was a defining moment that reinforced my belief in the power of communication.

## Giving Back Through Philanthropy

One of my most fulfilling decisions was donating all proceeds from my book sales to the TANKER Foundation, an NGO dedicated to supporting those in need. This experience showed me that creativity can serve a greater purpose, and that success is most meaningful when it helps others.

## The Role of 21K School

21K School has provided the flexibility and support I needed to balance my academics with my passions. The school's self-paced learning approach allowed me to dedicate time to my books, karate, and public speaking without compromising my studies. The encouragement from my facilitators gave me the confidence to push boundaries and dream big.

## Looking to the Future

As I continue to grow, I want to inspire others to pursue their passions fearlessly. Whether through writing, martial arts, or public speaking, my journey is a testament to perseverance, creativity, and kindness.

To my fellow learners: **Embrace challenges, think beyond limits, and always stay true to yourself. The world needs your unique voice and talents.**

**49**

## KANISHKA ALLURU

# Hitting the Bullseye: A Journey in Archery

### Finding My Passion

Hi, I'm Kanishka Alluru, a Grade 9 learner, and my journey in archery has been one of perseverance, discipline, and self-discovery. When I picked up my first bow and arrow, I had no idea that it would become such a defining part of my life. Archery has challenged me in ways I never imagined, pushing me to stay focused, improve my technique, and develop a champion's mindset.

### My First Major Victory

One of my proudest moments was at the MINI Nationals in 2018, my first-ever national competition. Competing against 1,392 participants, I won gold and silver medals, and my team, representing Andhra Pradesh, became state champions. That victory made me realize that with hard work, focus, and relentless practice, success is possible. It was the turning point that deepened my commitment to the sport.

### The Road to Mastery

Since that first competition, I have participated in over 70 tournaments, including 15+ national championships, 25+ state-level meets, and 30+ district competitions. I have earned more than 25 medals and certificates, including 1 gold, 2 silver, and 1 bronze. Each competition has been a stepping stone, teaching me the importance of patience, endurance, and adaptability.

## Facing Setbacks and Rising Stronger

In 2024, I encountered one of the biggest challenges of my career - I had to completely change my shooting technique. The transition was overwhelming, and my accuracy suffered. It was a frustrating phase, filled with self-doubt and setbacks. At one point, I considered stepping away from archery. However, after taking a short break to reflect, I returned with a renewed mindset and determination. I worked harder than ever, refining my skills and improving my scores. That struggle taught me a crucial lesson: growth happens in moments of difficulty, and setbacks are just opportunities to come back stronger.

## The Role of 21K School

Balancing archery with academics has been another challenge, but 21K School made it possible. The flexible learning schedule allowed me to dedicate time to my training while keeping up with my studies. My facilitators' support and encouragement made a huge difference. In Grade 8, I was invited to the Rising Achievers event, where I shared my journey. In Grade 9, I participated in the LIT Fest panel discussion, which improved my public speaking and confidence.

## Looking to the Future

Archery has shaped me into a stronger, more disciplined, and focused individual. As I continue to train and compete, I aim to perfect my technique and reach greater heights in national and international competitions. My dream is to represent India and inspire young athletes to pursue their passions fearlessly.

To my fellow learners: **Perseverance and passion will take you farther than you ever imagined. Keep aiming for your goals, and when you hit that bullseye, you'll know it was all worth it.**

**50**

## KEYA HATKAR

# Writing the Future: A Story of Resilience and Creativity

### My Journey as a Young Author

Hi, I'm Keya Hatkar, a Grade 8 learner at 21K School in Mumbai, India. My journey has been shaped by writing, art, coding, podcasting, YouTube, and singing - but more than anything, I am a storyteller. Writing is my way of expressing my thoughts, advocating for change, and inspiring others.

### Achievements in Writing and Beyond

My writing journey has been nothing short of incredible. I was honored as India's No. 1 Best Entrepreneur Author and Best-Selling Author at BriBooks NYAF for two consecutive years for my books Dancing on My Wheels and I M POSSIBLE!. Winning the Global Writing Prodigy Award and ORDI Rare Star Award strengthened my commitment to creative expression. However, my greatest honor came when I received the Pradhan Mantri Rashtriya Bal Puraskar 2025, India's highest civilian award for children.

### Turning Challenges into Strength

Living with Spinal Muscular Atrophy, an 80% physical disability, has not defined my journey - it has empowered me to advocate for inclusivity and awareness. Through my books and initiatives like I M Possible & SMAART, I raise awareness about rare diseases and resilience. I want my story to inspire children facing similar challenges to believe in themselves and never give up.

## A Strong Support System

My single mom and elder sister have been my pillars of strength. They have always reminded me that nothing is impossible, and their unwavering support has given me the confidence to face life's challenges head-on. Their belief in me, along with the encouragement from teachers, friends, and well-wishers, has shaped my resilience and determination.

## The Role of 21K School

21K School has played an invaluable role in my journey. Unlike traditional schools, 21K School provided me with an inclusive, tech-based platform where my abilities shone brighter than my disabilities. My English facilitator, Mary Ma'am, and the entire 21K community nurtured my talent and connected me with opportunities like BriBooks NYAF, which propelled me into the world of writing.

Since joining 21K School, I have grown not just as a writer but also as a learner leader. Writing has become my voice, my platform, and my way of driving change. With my school's support, I am working on translating my books into multiple Indian languages to reach a wider audience and spread awareness further.

## Looking to the Future

My goal is to continue writing, advocating for inclusivity, and making an impact through my words. I believe that stories have the power to change the world, and I want to use mine to inspire others to embrace their potential and push past limitations.

To my fellow learners: **Believe in your abilities, defy limitations, and never give up. No dream is too big if you have the courage to chase it.**

# 51

## S. J. LAKSHIN

# Harmony of Code and Strings: A Journey of Music & Innovation

### A Dual Passion

Hi, I'm Lakshin, a Grade 7 learner from Chennai, India, studying under the British Pathway at 21K School. My journey is a fusion of two worlds that might seem different but are deeply connected in my life - music and technology. These two passions have shaped who I am and have fueled my drive for creativity and innovation.

### The Rhythm of Music

From an early age, I found comfort in music. Learning to play the violin has been one of my greatest joys. Each note I play is like telling a story - one filled with emotion, discipline, and expression. Alongside the violin, I have also explored the keyboard, composing my own melodies that help me unwind. Music is more than a hobby; it is my personal escape and a way to communicate beyond words.

### A Deep Dive into Coding

While music nurtures my creativity, technology and coding fuel my curiosity. I have always been fascinated by how things work, and programming became my way of understanding and creating solutions. One of my proudest achievements was developing a health-monitoring application using Raspberry Pi and Thonny programming. This innovation allows users to track their pulse, breathing rate, and corpuscle levels from their homes. The experience of blending technology with a real-world solution was a defining moment in my journey.

## The Challenge of Balancing Passions

Juggling academics, music, and coding hasn't always been easy. There were times when preparing for the Science Olympiad while rehearsing for a musical performance felt overwhelming. However, I learned an important lesson: time management is key. With my father's guidance, I created a structured schedule that allowed me to dedicate time to each passion without feeling burnt out. This skill has helped me grow as a learner, musician, and innovator.

## The Role of 21K School

One of the biggest reasons I have been able to pursue both my passions successfully is 21K School. The school's flexibility and personalized learning approach have allowed me to balance my studies with extracurricular activities. Events like the Literary Fest and Mathalon have encouraged my creativity and problem-solving skills. The mentoring sessions at 21K School helped me overcome my fear of public speaking, boosting my confidence while presenting projects or performing in concerts.

## Looking to the Future

As I continue to learn and grow, my dream is to become a space scientist, working on technologies that solve real-world challenges beyond Earth. At the same time, I want to continue my journey in music, perhaps even leading a band one day. My inspirations, my violin coach, Sundar Pichai, and Nambi Narayanan, remind me that dedication and curiosity can lead to incredible achievements.

To my fellow learners: **Stay curious, keep dreaming, and never give up. Every challenge is a lesson, and every step you take brings you closer to your goals.**

**52**

# LAKSHYA SHREE P

# A Journey of Growth and Confidence

## Overcoming My Struggles

Hi, I'm Lakshya Shree P, a Grade 7 learner at 21K School in Bangalore, India. My story is one of transformation - one that took me from being a shy learner, afraid of math and public speaking, to becoming a confident debater, researcher, and aspiring diplomat.

## Facing My Fears

Math was once my biggest fear. The numbers seemed like an unsolvable puzzle, leaving me frustrated. However, instead of giving up, I challenged myself. Hours of practice and persistence paid off when I scored 100% in the Ramanujan Math Competition. That moment showed me that even our biggest weaknesses can become our strengths with the right mindset.

Similarly, public speaking terrified me. The thought of standing in front of an audience made me nervous. But as I kept participating in Model United Nations (MUN) events, I found my voice. One of my proudest achievements was winning 2nd place as the Delegate of Iraq at MUN 2024. This experience transformed me into someone who now finds power in speaking up and debating global issues.

## Exploring My Passions

Beyond academics, I have found joy in cycling and basketball. Cycling gives me space to think and reflect, while basketball teaches me teamwork and strategy.

One of my most fulfilling moments was hosting an eco-workshop with my classmates, where we creatively reused old materials to build new, useful items. The experience reinforced my belief that just like objects, people too have hidden potential waiting to be unlocked.

## The Role of 21K School

Joining 21K School was a turning point in my life. The school provided me with personalized lesson plans, a supportive learning environment, and mentors who believed in me. My facilitators encouraged me to see challenges as opportunities and fears as stepping stones to success. Their guidance helped me evolve into the confident and ambitious learner I am today.

## Looking Ahead

My dreams are big, and I am ready to chase them. I hope to study diplomacy or law at Harvard or NYU, using my skills to create a positive impact on the world. The lessons I have learned - critical thinking, perseverance, and self-belief - will be the foundation of my future.

To my fellow learners: **Every challenge is an opportunity to shine. Trust yourself, embrace your unique journey, and never stop striving for excellence.**

This is just the beginning of my story, and I'm excited for the chapters yet to come!

**53**

# MAHITHA NAIDU SURISETTY

# A Journey of Grit and Glory: My Story

## The Challenge That Defined Me

Hi, I'm Mahitha Naidu Surisetty from Bengaluru, India. My journey is not just about badminton or academics - it's about resilience, overcoming challenges, and proving that determination can defy all odds. My life took a major turn when, at just six years old, I was diagnosed with Type 1 Diabetes. At first, I didn't fully understand what it meant, but over time, frequent blood sugar checks, insulin injections, and strict diets became my reality.

## Finding Strength in Sports

Despite the daily challenges, I discovered my escape on the badminton court. The moment I stepped onto the court, everything else faded away. My focus was solely on the shuttle, my opponent, and the game. Training was intense, and balancing my health, school, and sports was not easy. Some days, fluctuating sugar levels made it difficult to focus and perform at my best, but I refused to let my condition define my limits.

## A Champion's Journey

By 2024, my hard work began to pay off. Winning Gold in Girls Doubles and Bronze in Girls Singles at the Yonex Sunrise All India Badminton Ranking Tournament in Dibrugarh, Assam, was a surreal moment. Standing on that podium was proof that my effort, struggles, and sacrifices were worth it. Soon after, I secured another Bronze in Girls Singles at the Karnataka State Mini Olympics at Kanteerava Stadium.

These victories were not just mine; they belonged to my parents, my coaches, and my unwavering support system.

## Overcoming Obstacles

Managing diabetes during tournaments was one of my toughest challenges. My family meticulously planned everything - from packing a cooking kit to ensuring I used an insulin pump during matches. Despite the emotional and physical toll, I kept reminding myself why I started this journey - to prove that I could overcome anything.

## The Role of 21K School

A huge part of my success is thanks to 21K School. Their flexible learning schedules allowed me to compete in tournaments without falling behind in academics. My teachers supported me with personalized lesson plans and counseling sessions, helping me balance my studies with my passion. Their constant encouragement reinforced my belief in myself.

## Looking to the Future

Through my journey, I've learned that resilience, discipline, and time management are key to success. My dream is to represent India on the international stage and earn a sports scholarship to pursue higher education while continuing my badminton career.

To my fellow learners: **Never give up. Challenges are not roadblocks; they are stepping stones to success. Believe in yourself, and you will achieve greatness.**

# 54

# Manishka Dubey

# From Tinkering to Transforming: My Story

## A Passion for Innovation

Hi, I'm Manishka Dubey, an 11-year-old innovator, author, and entrepreneur from Jodhpur, Rajasthan. My journey began when I was just five years old, exploring the fascinating world of STEM, robotics, and coding. What started as curiosity soon turned into an insatiable passion for creating, inventing, and problem-solving.

## Game-Changing Inventions

One of my proudest achievements is the Smart Self Tutor Device, a revolutionary tool designed to empower visually impaired children with accessible education. Witnessing how my invention changed lives was a humbling experience. Another breakthrough was the Kids Safety Band, which gained international recognition for its ability to enhance child safety. These inventions earned me prestigious awards, including the NCERT Special Award and multiple gold prizes at international innovation forums.

## The Journey as an Author

I wanted to inspire other young minds to embrace STEM and innovation, which led me to write Tinker to Techie. This book chronicles my journey, sharing insights, challenges, and the importance of thinking fearlessly. Writing and publishing this book was an empowering experience, helping me reach more young learners with the message that age is no barrier to success.

## The Challenge of Balancing Academics and Innovation

Managing academics, innovation, and writing is no easy task. There were moments when understanding complex scientific concepts felt overwhelming, but I never let frustration stop me. Instead, I treated challenges as learning opportunities. My biggest supporters - my family, mentors, and friends - reminded me that no dream is too big when you believe in yourself.

## The Role of 21K School

21K School has been instrumental in shaping my journey. The flexible online learning structure allowed me to pursue my passions while excelling academically. My facilitators encouraged me to participate in Olympiads, present at global forums, and contribute to platforms like the Literary Fest. These experiences gave me the confidence to take my work to the international stage.

## Breaking Barriers in STEM

Looking ahead, my mission is clear - I want to break stereotypes in STEM and encourage more girls to explore science and technology. I aim to continue solving real-world problems through innovation and making a positive impact on society.

## Looking to the Future

Reflecting on my journey, I feel an overwhelming sense of gratitude and determination. To anyone reading this, I want to say: Never underestimate the power of curiosity and resilience. Every small step you take brings you closer to your dreams.

To my fellow learners: **The road to success is paved with challenges, but it's also where the most beautiful discoveries are made. Dream big, take risks, and keep innovating!**

# 55

# MANN KOTHARI

# Leaping to Glory: My Gymnastics Journey

## Discovering My Passion

Hi, I'm Mann Kothari, a passionate gymnast, and my journey has been one of hard work, sacrifice, and relentless belief. It all began when I was five years old in Singapore, where I tried gymnastics for the first time. My parents noticed my curiosity and desire to challenge myself, and that moment set me on the path to pursuing gymnastics seriously.

## Training Across the World

After moving to Mumbai, I joined the Prabodhankar Thackeray Krida Sankul (PTKS) Elite Gymnastics Academy, where I was mentored by Coach Vishal Katakdound. He taught me an important lesson: "The body follows the mind." These words became the foundation of my training, shaping my discipline and focus. Inspired by Kohei Uchimura, I realized that gymnastics was not just about winning - it was about becoming the best version of myself.

To refine my skills, I trained at the South Essex Gymnastics Club (SEGC) in the UK under Coaches Anthony Wise and Scott Hann MBE. The international exposure helped me tackle weaknesses and polish my routines. I also trained at Infinity Gymnastics Club in Pune, where state-of-the-art equipment allowed me to push my limits further.

## Achievements and Recognition

In 2023, I was honored to be selected as a Khelo India Scholar, a pivotal moment that provided me with resources and training opportunities at the highest level.

Winning the Junior National Championship in 2024-25 was another dream come true. Claiming the All-Around title and silver in the Team Competition for Maharashtra reinforced my belief that my hard work was paying off.

Competing at the 5th Khelo India Youth Games (2023), where I secured a silver medal, was another significant milestone. However, I know that the journey does not end here - my ultimate goal is to represent India at the 2028 or 2032 Olympics.

## The Role of 21K School

Balancing rigorous training with academics was a challenge, but 21K School's flexible schedule made it possible. Their supportive learning environment allowed me to keep up with my studies while training for national and international competitions. The encouragement from my facilitators helped me stay motivated and focused on both gymnastics and education.

## Looking to the Future

My dream is to inspire young gymnasts to believe in themselves and work tirelessly toward their goals. Gymnastics has taught me that every fall is just a step toward the next big leap. I will continue training, refining my skills, and striving to make India proud on the global stage.

To my fellow learners: **Dream big, work hard, and never stop believing in yourself. The best is yet to come!**

# 56

## MARIAM SHAIKH

# The Journey of Strength and Persistence

### Discovering My Strength

Hi, I'm Mariam Shaikh, a dedicated karate champion and learner at 21K School in Goa, India. My journey in karate began when I was just five years old, and today, I am proud to have won multiple gold medals in Kata and Kumite at the Indo-Sri Lankan Open Karate Championship and the TKAG District Karate Championship 2024. However, my journey is about more than just winning medals - it's about discipline, perseverance, and personal growth.

### Balancing Karate and Academics

Being a young athlete comes with challenges, especially when it comes to balancing training and schoolwork. Karate demands intense practice sessions, and there are days when I feel exhausted, overwhelmed, and drained. However, I have learned that time management and perseverance are key to excelling in both academics and sports.

At times, waking up early for school after late-night training sessions felt impossible. But I reminded myself that champions push through difficulties and never quit. The challenges I faced only made me more determined to become the best version of myself.

### The Role of 21K School

21K School has been a pillar of support in my journey. My teacher, Ms. Divya, introduced me to the concept of "Habits of Mind", which helped me develop persistence, focus, and resilience.

These lessons guided me through tough moments in both karate and academics, reminding me to never give up, no matter how difficult things get.

The school's flexible learning approach allowed me to catch up on lessons I missed due to training. The availability of recorded sessions and study materials in PDF format ensured that I never fell behind. Additionally, the counseling sessions provided by 21K School helped me manage stress and maintain a positive mindset.

## Looking to the Future

My dream is to become the World Karate Champion and continue excelling in academics. I know that achieving this goal will require dedication, discipline, and continuous hard work, but I am ready for the challenge.

I am deeply grateful to my parents, coach, teachers, and school for believing in me and providing the support I need to chase my dreams. This is just the beginning, and I am excited for what lies ahead.

To my fellow learners: **"It's not about being better than someone else; it's about being better than you were the day before."**

Keep striving, keep growing, and success will follow!

**57**

## MEGAN FRANCIS

# Riding Through Life: Lessons from the Open Road

### A Life on Two Wheels

Hi, I'm Megan Francis, and my journey is anything but ordinary. The hum of a motorbike engine, the wind against my face, and the endless road ahead - that's where I feel most alive. Growing up in Bengaluru, India, my life was filled with school, art, music, and books, but none of these could match the exhilaration of riding my motorbike, Charlie the Harley.

### Exploring the Unexplored

With my parents, Francis Binny Jose and Patsy Teresa Jose, I have traveled to every corner of India. From the snowy heights of Khardung La to the sunlit beaches of Kanyakumari, every journey has been an adventure. My proudest moment came when Harley-Davidson awarded me the 1,00,000-kilometre patch in Goa, making me the youngest rider in the world to achieve this distinction.

### Facing Challenges Head-On

Balancing academics with travel was not easy. There were days when we reached a hotel past midnight, or I found myself in places with no internet connectivity. Yet, I never let these obstacles hold me back. My parents and grandparents played a crucial role in keeping me motivated, teaching me that with determination and creativity, anything is possible.

### The Role of 21K School

21K School became my academic anchor. Its flexible remote learning system allowed me to attend classes from anywhere. Whenever I missed a lecture due to connectivity issues or exhaustion from a ride, I relied on recorded lessons to stay on track. The unwavering support from my facilitators helped me balance my education with my passion for riding.

### Lessons from the Road

Traveling has taught me to adapt to the unexpected - whether it's finding shelter under a tree when there's no accommodation or surviving on minimal food during long rides. India's diverse cultures, cuisines, and landscapes have broadened my perspective and deepened my understanding of the world.

### Looking to the Future

My dreams extend beyond India. I envision a future where I can ride across the world, connecting with people and collecting stories from every corner of the globe. Riding is not just my passion - it is my way of understanding life, one mile at a time.

To my fellow learners: **"Life is like a road trip - enjoy each day and don't carry too much baggage."**

The road ahead is full of promise, and I can't wait to see where it leads.

**58**

## NAMAN KATOCH

# Big Dreams in a Small Package: A Young Achiever's Story

## Creativity and Curiosity

Hi, I'm Naman Katoch, a KG1 learner from Mohali, India. My life is filled with drawing, coloring, writing, running, and building things with blocks. These hobbies are more than just fun - they fuel my imagination and creativity, helping me express myself in unique ways.

## Rising as a Performer

This year, I achieved something special by participating in national-level competitions organized by the Child Dream Booster Hub, supported by the Government of India. I won the Live National Singing Contest, receiving a trophy and a medal. I was also recognized as a Super Performer in the Live National Poem Recitation Competition, earning another medal. These achievements made me feel proud and excited, proving that with dedication and hard work, anything is possible.

## The Challenge of Performing Live

Preparing for these competitions wasn't easy. With only two days to practice, I had to focus and work harder than ever. My mom and maternal grandfather stood by me every step of the way, helping me rehearse and boosting my confidence.

## The Role of 21K School

My school, 21K School, has been a huge part of my journey. My facilitators encouraged me, giving me the confidence to do my best.

The mentoring sessions they organized kept me motivated, and their belief in me made all the difference. Knowing that my teachers were proud of me pushed me to perform even better.

## Lessons from the Stage

Performing live in front of an audience was scary at first, but it taught me important lessons about staying calm and confident under pressure. Now, I enjoy being on stage and look forward to new challenges.

## Looking to the Future

One thing I've learned is the power of positivity and believing in myself. I often remind myself, "I am there for you. I believe in you. I think I can." These words keep me strong and determined to keep growing and learning.

I am grateful to my family and my school facilitators for their unwavering support. Their encouragement has been the foundation of my achievements. As I grow, I want to continue working hard, learning, and exploring all the exciting opportunities life has to offer.

To my fellow learners: **"Every positive thought is a silent prayer which will change your life."**

I truly believe in the magic of positive thinking, and I can't wait to see where my dreams take me next!

**59**

## NANDAN DAS

# Racing Beyond Limits: A Champion's Journey

### The Thrill of Speed

Hi, I'm Nandan Das, a Grade 6 learner from 21K School's British Pathway in Bangalore, India. My world revolves around two things - cycling and motorsports. Ever since I was four years old, I have been drawn to the rush of speed, the challenge of the race, and the joy of crossing the finish line. What started as a childhood hobby soon turned into a professional pursuit, where I have now earned over 60 podium finishes in Mountain Bike (MTB) and Supercross events.

### Achievements That Drive Me Forward

Competing at the National Supercross Championship and securing 3rd place was one of my biggest milestones. Racing against India's best riders was both thrilling and humbling, pushing me to train harder and improve my skills. Winning a silver medal in the Bangalore District Cycling Championship and finishing 6th at the Karnataka State MTB Championship are achievements that reflect the countless hours of dedication I have put into my training.

### Overcoming Obstacles

The journey to success has been far from easy. Balancing academics with professional sports is a constant challenge. My days begin early with intense track sessions, evenings are dedicated to schoolwork, and weekends are packed with competitions. Injuries are also part of the journey - from minor bruises to serious fractures - but they have only made me stronger.

I've learned that setbacks are temporary, but perseverance lasts forever.

## The Role of 21K School

21K School has played a key role in my success. The school's flexible learning model allows me to travel for competitions without falling behind in academics. The constant encouragement from my facilitators has helped me balance both worlds, and their mentorship has been invaluable in my growth.

## Looking to the Future

I aspire to represent India at the international level in Supercross and MTB Championships. My dream is to bring global recognition to Indian motorsports and cycling. Beyond racing, I am fascinated by sports science and the mechanics of peak performance, and I hope to explore this field further.

To my fellow learners: **Never stop chasing your dreams, no matter how tough the journey gets. Every challenge is an opportunity to grow, and the race isn't over until you decide to stop. Keep pushing forward!**

# 60

# Navtej Manjunathan

# Aiming for the Top: The Road to Tennis Excellence

## The Beginning of a Dream

Hi, I'm Navtej Manjunathan, a 14-year-old tennis player from Bangalore, India, currently training in Warsaw, Poland. My journey with tennis began when I was 10 years old, and since then, it has been a story of passion, perseverance, and ambition.

## Reaching New Heights in Tennis

This year has been a turning point for me. I started with a wildcard entry into a tournament, where I won my first trophy of the year. Another major milestone was playing in my first Under-16 tournament - I won the semifinals 6-0, 6-3 against the top seed, a match that tested my resilience. Although I lost in the finals, the experience taught me valuable lessons about handling pressure and competing against stronger players.

One of my proudest moments was playing in my first Under-18 tournament at just 14 years old. Competing against older, more experienced players was tough, but it helped me level up my game. More recently, I finished as the runner-up in an Under-14 tournament, proving to myself that consistency and preparation are key to long-term success.

## Challenges and Growth

Moving to Poland for training came with its own set of challenges. Adapting to new playing surfaces, unfamiliar training techniques, and a different climate took time.

There were days when I doubted myself, but each challenge only made me more determined. With feedback from my coaches, support from my family, and my own relentless drive, I continued to grow.

## The Role of 21K School

Balancing my intense training schedule with academics would have been impossible without 21K School. Their self-paced learning model and resources like ATL and HOM helped me stay organized. The school's support made sure I could focus on both my game and my studies without compromise.

## Looking Ahead

My ultimate goal is to become World No. 1 in singles tennis. This year, I am aiming to break into the top 10 in Under-16 rankings in Poland. Alongside tennis, I am committed to excelling academically, aiming to do well in my 9th-grade studies and pass my 10th-grade exams with flying colors.

To my fellow learners: **Hard work pays off. Push yourself beyond your limits, and in a couple of years, you'll look back and see how far you've come. Stay dedicated, stay hungry, and never stop aiming for the top!**

**61**

## Nithila Das

# From Pedals to Power: From Cycling to Motorsports

### The Thrill of Speed

Hi, I'm Nithila Das, and speed has always been my passion. It started as friendly sibling rivalry, racing against my brother, but soon evolved into something much bigger. My journey began on the rugged trails of Karnataka, where I discovered my love for mountain biking (MTB). There was something exhilarating about tackling tough terrains and steep descents - it wasn't just about winning races, it was about pushing my limits.

### Conquering the Cycling World

In 2020, I won the Karnataka State MTB Championship, a defining moment in my cycling career. The victory wasn't just about the gold medal - it was about proving to myself that I had the mental and physical endurance to compete at the highest level. Soon after, I joined the Trailblazers Racing Team, determined to inspire other young cyclists in India.

### The Shift to Motorsports

While cycling was my first love, I was drawn to the roar of engines and the thrill of speed on two wheels. In 2022, I took a bold leap into the TVS One-Make Championship, transitioning from mountain trails to high-speed racetracks. The learning curve was steep, but I quickly adapted. My biggest achievement came when I was crowned the Fastest Girl in India at the FIM MiniGP, proving that I could hold my own in international motorsports.

## Overcoming Challenges

Balancing cycling, motorsports, and academics has been a constant challenge. Training for two demanding sports requires mental focus, stamina, and adaptability. Some days, I find myself switching between cycling trails and racetracks, but I have learned to embrace the grind. Every competition, whether on a bicycle or a motorcycle, is a new lesson in resilience.

## The Role of 21K School

Managing school and sports would not have been possible without 21K School. Their flexible learning schedule allows me to train intensively while keeping up with my studies. The encouragement from my facilitators and peers has been instrumental in keeping me motivated.

## Looking to the Future

My journey is far from over. I want to continue breaking barriers in motorsports, paving the way for more girls in the industry. Whether on a mountain trail or a race track, my goal remains the same: to push my limits and inspire others to chase their dreams fearlessly.

To my fellow learners: **Dare to dream, push boundaries, and never let anyone tell you that you can't achieve greatness. The road ahead is yours to conquer!**

**62**

## NITYA V

# Designing My Future: A Story of Passion and Creativity

### The Art of Innovation

Hi, I'm Nitya V, a senior secondary learner in the Indian Pathway at 21K School, and my world revolves around art, photography, writing, poetry, and reading. Creativity is the lens through which I view the world, and my passion for design has shaped my journey.

### Achievements That Define Me

Over the last two years, I have dedicated myself to preparing for design entrance exams, and the results have been incredibly rewarding:

- Rank 18 in UCEED
- Rank 187 in NID
- Rank 52 in NIFT
- 2nd place in the DH23 Design Hackathon by DQ Labs

Beyond academics, I have explored real-world design applications, including:

- Designing a logo for a bakery company
- Creating an album cover for the Inter IIT Sports Anthem Release 2024-25
- Volunteering for ICORD 25, an international design conference

Each of these experiences has reinforced my belief that design is not just about aesthetics - it is about solving problems and telling stories.

## Overcoming Challenges

Balancing academics, entrance exams, and personal projects has been demanding. Studying from home sometimes felt isolating and monotonous, making it hard to stay motivated. However, my family, friends, and peers played a crucial role in keeping me grounded. Their support reminded me of the importance of balance - between study and play, creativity and structure.

## The Role of 21K School

21K School has been a major part of my success. The school's structured curriculum and flexible schedules allowed me to prepare for competitive exams while staying on top of my academics. The support from facilitators and interactive learning sessions helped create a sense of community, making my learning journey more engaging and fulfilling.

## Looking to the Future

My goal is to continue pushing creative boundaries and using design to make a positive impact. Whether it's through psychology, environmental science, or product design, I want to merge art with functionality to create meaningful solutions for the world.

To my fellow learners: **Embrace your creativity, stay curious, and believe in your ability to innovate. The future is a blank canvas - paint it with your dreams!**

**63**

# NOUMAAN SHAIKH

# The Abacus Prodigy: Calculating My Way to Success

## A Journey into Numbers

Hi, I'm Noumaan Shaikh, an 8-year-old Grade 2 learner, and numbers are my playground. My journey with the abacus began in 2021 at Wisdom Brains Academy, and it has been an incredible adventure in problem-solving, speed, and mental agility.

## Becoming a Champion

For three consecutive years, I clinched 1st place in the International Abacus Championships. But in 2024, the competition got tougher, and I finished in 3rd place. While I was initially disappointed, I realized that true champions don't quit - they rise, learn, and come back stronger. My goal now is to reclaim my top spot next year.

## The Early Challenges

When I started learning the abacus in UKG, even simple addition and subtraction felt challenging. My mother, my biggest supporter, was unsure if I would grasp the concepts. However, watching my older sister - an abacus champion herself - motivate me to keep practicing. With daily effort and persistence, I began solving calculations with speed and accuracy.

## The Power of the Abacus

The abacus is more than just numbers - it's a tool that trains the brain. Through this journey, I have gained:

- Fast Calculation: I can solve problems faster than most of my friends - and sometimes even faster than a calculator!

- Improved Memory: My ability to remember numbers, patterns, and school lessons has sharpened significantly.

- Focus and Concentration: The abacus requires deep attention, helping me improve my study habits and learning ability.

- Confidence: Competing in championships has boosted my belief in myself.

## The Role of 21K School

21K School has supported my love for learning. The flexible learning system ensures I can train for my competitions while keeping up with academics. My teachers have encouraged me at every step, reminding me that hard work and perseverance always lead to success.

## Looking to the Future

I believe that if every child in India learned the abacus, we would sharpen our minds, improve our problem-solving skills, and build a stronger, more innovative nation. This is how I connect my abacus journey with Swarnim Bharat - a future where India leads in science, technology, and innovation.

To my fellow learners: **Never give up, no matter how hard it seems. Keep learning, keep growing, and you'll become a champion in your own way.**

**64**

## OM VAINAV SHAIVA P

# From the Nets to the Field: My Journey with Cricket

### A Dream on the Pitch

Hi, I'm Om Vainav Shaiva P, an 11th-grade learner from Bengaluru, India, and cricket is my life. I was honored to represent Bangalore City XI in the KSCA Under-16 Inter Zonal Tournament for 2024-25. Out of 1,024 cricketers who came for selection trials, only 68 were chosen, and I was one of them. My next goal? To make it to the state team.

### Juggling Cricket and Academics

This achievement did not come easy. My 10th-grade board exams coincided with crucial league matches, which meant I was studying for exams one day and playing matches the next. The pressure was immense, but I was determined to balance both.

My routine was intense - waking up early for net practice, rushing to schoolwork, and then heading to evening training. Long hours of traveling across the city for matches added to the challenge. At times, I felt exhausted, but my love for cricket kept me going.

### The Role of 21K School

21K School was a game-changer for me. Without its flexibility, balancing cricket and studies would have been nearly impossible. Being able to carry my education with me as I traveled for matches gave me the freedom to train without worrying about missing out on lessons. The NIOS syllabus, which reduces academic pressure, allowed me to focus on both my game and my studies.

## Lessons from Cricket

Cricket has taught me more than just technique - it has instilled in me discipline, resilience, and mental strength. The sport has made me:

- **Physically stronger:** Training under the sun for hours has built my stamina and endurance.

- **Mentally resilient:** Cricket has taught me that wins and losses are part of the game, but perseverance is what matters most.

- **A better communicator:** Playing with teammates from different backgrounds has helped me understand different cultures and perspectives.

## Looking to the Future

I am determined to keep improving my skills and one day represent India on the international cricket field. My journey has just begun, and I know that with dedication, training, and the right mindset, I will achieve my goals.

To my fellow learners: **There are no shortcuts to success. Keep practicing, stay focused, and never stop believing in yourself. Your dreams are worth the effort!**

# 65

## Phalak Mathur

# From Shy to Confident: My Growth Journey at 21K School

### A Transformation Begins

Hi, I'm Phalak Mathur, and my journey at 21K School has been nothing short of transformative. When I joined in Grade 9 in 2022, I was a quiet and shy learner, unsure of how to balance academics with my other passions. Little did I know that this school would not just shape my education but also help me grow into a confident and ambitious learner.

### Embracing New Opportunities

One of the most valuable aspects of 21K School has been its structured curriculum and supportive environment. From guiding me through the NIOS system to preparing me for entrance exams, the constant support from my teachers has been exceptional. Even though I study from home, the school fosters a strong sense of community, with breakout rooms, group discussions, and collaborative projects, making learning engaging and interactive.

When I first joined, I hesitated to step out of my comfort zone. However, over time, I began to embrace academic and extracurricular opportunities. A turning point for me was participating in the Lit Fest panel discussion, which significantly boosted my public speaking skills. Since then, I have confidently taken part in various school events, learning to express my ideas in front of audiences and peer groups.

## Achievements and Personal Growth

My time at 21K School has been filled with achievements, including multiple certificates and recognitions. These accolades serve as a reminder of how far I've come. However, beyond awards, the most valuable skill I've developed is time management. Balancing academics, hobbies, and social life is a challenge, especially with board exams and entrance test preparations. Yet, I have learned to stay grounded by making time for family, friends, and self-care, which helps me stay motivated and focused.

## The Power of Support

None of this progress would have been possible without my family, friends, and peers. My family has been my foundation, encouraging me to stay focused while reminding me to take breaks when needed. Conversations with friends provide emotional support, while my peers at 21K School have played a crucial role in my journey. Through collaborative learning, teamwork, and shared experiences, we support each other in both academics and personal growth.

## Looking to the Future

As I prepare for Grade 11 and 12, I am excited about how 21K School is shaping my future. The flexible schedules allow me to dedicate time to entrance exams while engaging in an enriching curriculum. The encouragement from my teachers, classmates, and facilitators has made learning effective and enjoyable.

Reflecting on my time at 21K School, I feel immense gratitude for the experiences and lessons I've gained. The journey has helped me become more confident, self-assured, and ready for the next chapter of my life.

To my fellow learners: **Step out of your comfort zone, embrace new experiences, and trust yourself - you are capable of more than you realize!**

# 66

## PRAJIN RAVIKUMAR

# A Cricket Journey of Dedication and Growth

**A Passion for Cricket**

Hi, I'm Prajin Ravikumar, and my journey at 21K School has been shaped by cricket, passion, and perseverance. From leading teams to achieving personal milestones, I have faced numerous challenges, but with dedication and the support of my family, coaches, and the 21K community, I have learned invaluable lessons along the way.

**The Road to Success**

Cricket has been my lifelong passion. I have been fortunate to achieve several milestones, including:

- Captaining both the Under-16 and Under-19 cricket teams
- Winning Player of the Match honors 9 times
- Receiving Best Batsman awards 11 times
- Scoring 1500 runs in a single season
- Accumulating 8000 runs over 263 innings

These milestones are not just numbers; they are a testament to my consistency and dedication, backed by countless hours of practice, discipline, and focus.

**Overcoming Challenges**

Balancing cricket with academics has been one of the toughest challenges. Long training sessions often clashed with exams, and managing time became stressful.

Additionally, physical injuries took a toll on my progress, forcing me to watch my team play from the sidelines. These moments were emotionally difficult, but I learned to stay calm under pressure and view setbacks as opportunities for growth.

To overcome these hurdles, I developed a strict time-management plan, ensuring I dedicated time to both academics and cricket. Injury prevention routines and mental conditioning techniques helped me recover faster and play stronger. I also practiced mindfulness and focus techniques, which were crucial in high-pressure matches.

## The Role of 21K School

The flexibility at 21K School was crucial to my success. The school's personalized lesson plans and recorded classes allowed me to focus on cricket without compromising my academics. The school also provided mentorship, group therapy, and personalized guidance, helping me set both short- and long-term goals.

At 21K School, I thrived not just as a learner but as an athlete. The school's support enabled me to build discipline, a growth mindset, and resilience, qualities that extend beyond the field.

## Looking to the Future

I have learned that success requires persistence and consistency - not just talent. My short-term goal is to represent India in the Under-19 cricket team, while my long-term dream is to become a nutritionist, helping athletes make informed health choices.

To my fellow learners: **Never give up on your dreams. Challenges will come, but it's how you respond that defines you. Embrace the journey, celebrate small victories, and keep striving for greatness!**

I am deeply grateful to my family, coaches, and the facilitators at 21K School for their unwavering support. Your belief in me has been instrumental in my growth.

# 67

# Prathamesh Sainath

# My Chess Journey: A Story of Passion and Perseverance

## A Lifelong Love for Chess

Hi, I'm Prathamesh Sainath, and chess has been an inseparable part of my life. It is a game of strategy, patience, and resilience, and through chess, I have learned lessons that go beyond the board. My journey began at an early age, and since then, I have competed at state, national, and international levels, constantly pushing my limits and striving for excellence.

## Achievements That Define Me

Over the years, I have had the privilege of winning multiple state championships, including Under-7, Under-9, Under-11, Under-13 (twice), and Under-15 titles. These victories led me to the national stage, where I achieved 3rd place in the Under-15 category and 2nd place in the Under-13 category. Each tournament, whether a win or a loss, has been a stepping stone in my journey.

## Overcoming Challenges

The road to success in chess has not been easy. Balancing 8-hour training sessions with academics required extreme discipline and time management. At one point, I struggled with a phase of video game addiction, which affected my focus. Additionally, overcoming stage fright and public speaking anxiety felt as challenging as defeating a grandmaster on the board.

To navigate these challenges, I built strict schedules, set clear priorities, and found ways to stay focused. Listening to music helped me stay calm, and my father's quiet confidence kept me motivated. My mother's unwavering belief in my potential pushed me to stay committed, reminding me that no dream is too big when backed by hard work and dedication.

## The Role of 21K School

Finding 21K School was a game-changer for me. The flexible learning schedule allowed me to excel in both chess and academics without feeling overwhelmed. My facilitators were incredibly supportive, especially Nidhi Ma'am, whose constant encouragement gave me the motivation to keep pushing forward.

## Looking to the Future

As I continue my chess journey, my ultimate goal is to become a world chess champion - not just for myself but for everyone who has supported me along the way. Chess has shaped me into a focused, strategic, and resilient individual, and I am excited about the future ahead.

To my fellow learners: **Success is not about avoiding failure; it is about learning from every challenge. Embrace every setback as an opportunity to grow, and never lose sight of your goals!**

# 68

# PRATYAKSHA SARASWAT

# A Journey of Music, Yoga and Growth

**The Power of Music and Movement**

Hi, I'm Pratyaksha Saraswat, a Grade 10 learner at 21K School in Delhi, and my world is filled with music, yoga, and creativity. Whether I am singing, composing, or practicing yoga, I find balance and inspiration in everything I do.

**Milestones That Shaped My Journey**

Looking back, I am proud of several accomplishments that have defined my growth:

- Composing and singing four original songs, some of which were launched by former President Ram Nath Kovind and writer Ruskin Bond.

- Receiving the Pratibha Samman Award from Anandiben Patel, Governor of Uttar Pradesh, and Dr. Mohan Bhagwat.

- Winning the 'My Life, My Yoga' contest, organized by the Government of India.

- Being interviewed by News 24 at just 10 years old, after launching my first song.

- Exploring creative writing and blackout poetry, earning recognition at my school's Literary Fest.

Overcoming Challenges

Balancing music, yoga, and academics was not easy. Some nights, I worked late on music production, and other days, I felt overwhelmed by exams and deadlines.

There were moments of self-doubt, where I questioned if I was doing enough, but I realized that challenges are part of the journey, not the end of it.

## The Role of 21K School

21K School played a crucial role in my growth. Its flexible learning structure allowed me to pursue my passions without sacrificing academics. My vocal teacher helped me build confidence, while my mother encouraged my yoga journey. My English teacher, Ms. Naaz Hafiz, pushed me to embrace literary excellence, and Ms. Supti Ghosh nurtured my creative side.

## Looking to the Future

As I continue to explore music, literature, and yoga, I want to inspire others to follow their passions fearlessly. My dream is to blend my love for the arts with a career that allows me to impact the world positively.

To my fellow learners: **Consistency and passion will take you further than you ever imagined. Keep learning, keep growing, and always follow your heart!**

# 69

## PRATYUSH

# Beyond Boundaries: Exploring, Learning, and Achieving

### A Journey of Exploration

Hi, I'm Pratyush, a learner of British 3AA at 21K School, currently residing in Toyohashi, Japan. My life is a mix of sports, academics, and cultural exploration. Whether it's cricket, dodgeball, soccer, chess, or karate, I believe in pushing my limits to excel in multiple fields.

### Achievements That Define Me

My journey has been filled with accomplishments that shaped me into who I am today. Some of my key milestones include:

Winning the Stunning Star Award at the Kana's Abacus Academy in 2023 and 2024, marking my excellence in Abacus competitions.

Earning my 12th-grade completion certificate in karate from the Shimoto Ikujun Karate Association in 2024, a significant recognition of my dedication and discipline.

Receiving a Certificate of Excellence at the Toyota International Festival Japanese Speech Contest in 2024, where I competed against participants from 12 different countries.

### Overcoming Challenges

Balancing academics with multiple extracurriculars has been challenging. Adapting to Japan's diverse climate affected my training schedules, and managing intensive karate practice while preparing for academic tests left me exhausted. However, I learned to manage my time effectively and push forward, even when it felt overwhelming.

## The Role of 21K School

One of the best things about 21K School is its flexibility. The online learning environment allowed me to attend classes from anywhere, ensuring that my education never suffered despite my packed schedule. The quizzes and interactive lessons sharpened my thinking skills, helping me stay ahead in both academics and extracurricular pursuits.

## Looking to the Future

This is just the beginning. I am excited to continue exploring new challenges, refining my skills, and pushing my boundaries. I aim to take my achievements beyond Japan and compete on an international stage.

To my fellow learners: **Believe in yourself, stay curious, and never stop learning. Greatness lies within you!**

# 70

# RAAJVEER PARAB

# Strength, Resilience, and Triumph in Judo

## Finding My Passion

Hi, I'm Raajveer Parab, and at just seven years old, I have already found my purpose and passion in the sport of Judo. What started as a martial art lesson soon became a journey of discipline, respect, and self-improvement.

## Achievements That Inspire Me

Within just ten months, I have competed in six major judo tournaments, earning recognition for my dedication:

- Bronze medal at the Sensei N.T. and M.N. Bangera Memorial Judo Championship in February 2024.

- Bronze medal at the Prof. Jigoro Kano Invitational Mumbai Judo Championship in August 2024.

- Silver medals at the Late Shri V.V. Bhat Memorial Inter-School Championship and Sports For All Tournament in September 2024.

- Gold medal at the VIBGYOR Airoli Inter-School Competition in October 2024, my biggest victory so far.

- Bronze medal at the VIBGYOR Goregaon VIVA Inter-School Competition, closing a successful year of competition.

## Lessons Learned Through Judo

Judo is more than just winning matches; it's about developing mental toughness and resilience. Competing in higher weight categories challenged me to refine my techniques and build my strength.

I have learned that slow progress is still progress, and every match is a lesson in perseverance.

## The Role of 21K School

My journey would not have been possible without the flexible learning system at 21K School. With support from facilitators and personalized learning plans, I have been able to balance my academics with my rigorous training schedule.

## Looking to the Future

Judo is more than just a sport - it is my way of life. I dream of inspiring others with my journey, proving that age is just a number when it comes to passion and hard work. I will continue training, improving, and competing with the goal of making it to national and international championships.

To my fellow learners: **Discipline, consistency, and perseverance will take you further than talent alone. Keep pushing forward, and success will follow!**

# 71

# Ravyanshi Singh

# A Journey of Dreams: Writing, Science, and Innovation

## The Passion That Drives Me

Hi, I'm Ravyanshi Singh, a Grade 6 learner from Singapore, studying in the Indian pathway at 21K School. My journey is one of exploration, passion, and perseverance. I believe that every day presents an opportunity to learn, grow, and inspire change.

## Writing as a Tool for Change

Writing is my greatest passion. Through storytelling and poetry, I raise awareness about child education, women's empowerment, and climate change. I have participated in talk shows and written books on science and climate change, which became bestsellers. One of my proudest moments was presenting my books to the Honourable President of India, Smt. Droupadi Murmu. Being recognized as the 7th Young Pioneer Author in 2024 by BriBooks was a defining milestone in my journey.

## Achievements in Science and Academics

Beyond writing, I am deeply involved in science and technology. Some of my greatest achievements include:

- International Rank 1 in the Indian School Talent Search Examination (ISTSE) for two consecutive years.
- National Rank 2 in the National Astronomical Challenge Olympiad.
- International Rank 3 in the World's Math Championship.
- Participation in NASA's asteroid-hunting program and the India AI Impact Festival.

These experiences have deepened my love for science, astronomy, and AI, pushing me to explore new horizons.

## Overcoming Challenges

Juggling academics, writing, and Olympiads was never easy. Late nights spent researching and writing took a toll on my health, but I found balance through mindfulness, sports, and structured planning. Tackling technical hurdles while learning AI taught me perseverance and adaptability.

## The Role of 21K School

My success would not have been possible without 21K School. The school's personalized learning environment and project-based curriculum helped me develop leadership skills and confidence. Events like the Literary Fest and Science Exhibition allowed me to showcase my talents and refine my creative thinking.

## Looking to the Future

Moving forward, I aspire to write more books on astronomy and geography, contribute to scientific research, and continue inspiring young minds to dream big. My journey has taught me that every challenge is an opportunity for growth.

To my fellow learners: **Take small steps toward your dreams, embrace challenges, and stay curious. Together, we can light up the world with courage and determination!**

# 72

# RIANA SARAF

# Exploring the World Through Art and Science

## A Young Mind Full of Imagination

Hi, I'm Riana Saraf, a Grade 3 learner from Milan, Italy, studying under the British Pathway at 21K School. My world is filled with art, music, LEGO, and science. These passions fuel my creativity and drive me to explore and learn in unique ways.

## Achievements That Inspire Me

My creative journey has led me to achieve some incredible milestones:

- Winning an art competition at age seven in 2022.
- Winning a Silver Medal at the World Science Championship in 2025, my first-ever science competition.

Participating in an international science championship was a new experience for me, and it taught me the value of perseverance and dedication.

## Overcoming Challenges

Competing at the world level meant stepping outside my comfort zone. I had to adapt to new learning methods and push myself harder than ever. There were moments when I felt overwhelmed, but I reminded myself that every challenge is a stepping stone to growth.

## The Role of 21K School

21K School has played an essential role in my learning journey. The flexible online learning model allowed me to attend classes from anywhere, ensuring I never missed a lesson. Personalized lesson plans, regular quizzes, and engaging teaching methods helped me excel in science and other subjects.

My mentor and class teacher, Akanksha Bhati Ma'am, was instrumental in helping me understand complex scientific concepts. Her teaching approach made learning fun, engaging, and impactful.

## Looking to the Future

Winning the Silver Medal at the World Science Championship has strengthened my love for science and innovation. My goal is to continue excelling in both academics and creative pursuits, using my imagination and curiosity to discover new possibilities.

To my fellow learners: **Find joy in learning, never stop asking questions, and embrace your creativity. The more curious you are, the more you will discover!**

# 73

# RIDHI SEHGAL

# Passion, Perseverance, and Purpose: Growth and Creativity

## A Multifaceted Journey

Hi, I'm Ridhi Sehgal, a Grade 12 learner from Gurugram, Haryana, with a wide array of interests spanning academics, sports, music, coding, and design. My journey has been about embracing challenges and discovering my true potential in various fields.

## Achievements That Define Me

Some of my proudest milestones include:

- Earning the 'Topper' badge in Computational Thinking and Python from IIT Madras, showcasing my analytical and problem-solving skills.

- Ranking among the top scorers in the IITM BS degree program, proving my dedication to academic excellence.

- Leading a blanket and rug collection drive for stray dogs, fulfilling a deep-seated desire to give back to the community.

- Exploring graphic design through Adobe Photoshop and After Effects, creating impactful visual content.

- Teaching permutations and combinations to my peers, refining my communication and mentoring abilities.

## Overcoming Challenges

Balancing academics and extracurriculars has been one of my biggest hurdles. Managing time efficiently while also dealing with stage fright and simplifying complex concepts tested my patience and adaptability.

However, I developed a structured approach to time management, collaborated with mentors and peers, and used creative learning techniques to make concepts more accessible.

**The Role of 21K School**

21K School provided me with the flexibility and academic rigor necessary to pursue my diverse interests. The school's interactive learning environment and personalized guidance enabled me to explore beyond textbooks and engage deeply in my passions.

**Looking to the Future**

As I move forward in my academic journey, I am committed to making a meaningful impact by combining my creativity, technical skills, and social consciousness. I hope to inspire others to embrace challenges, explore their potential, and never stop growing.

To my fellow learners: **Resilience, creativity, and a willingness to learn will take you further than you can imagine. Stay curious and keep pushing boundaries!**

# 74

## RITVIK ZYAN

# My Journey of Creativity and Growth

### A Young Creator in the Making

Hi, I'm Ritvik Zyan, a Grade 2 learner at 21K School in Bangalore, India. My journey has been an exciting blend of creativity, challenges, and achievements. From photography to reel-making, I've discovered the joy of turning ideas into reality.

### How It All Began

It all started with a simple question: How do people create amazing edits and reels? That curiosity sparked my passion for photo editing and video creation. At first, understanding the tools felt overwhelming, but I kept experimenting, and soon, I started creating magical edits with animations, slow-motion effects, and creative transitions.

### Achievements That Inspire Me

Looking back, I feel proud of what I've accomplished:

- Winning awards for handwriting, state-level art, drawing, and fancy dress in Grade 1.
- Receiving the prestigious Kala Bhushan Award after winning the national creative reel-making competition.

These achievements symbolize my dedication, self-motivation, and love for learning.

## Overcoming Challenges

Balancing hobbies, studies, and assignments was not always easy. I struggled with time management and complex concepts, but I developed a routine that included breaks, snacks, and music to recharge my energy. Over time, I improved and realized that consistency is the key to success.

## The Role of 21K School

21K School played a huge role in my journey. The Habits of Mind (HOMs) program, interactive resources, and encouraging facilitators helped me build confidence and push my boundaries.

## Looking Ahead

I am excited to continue exploring my creative interests and achieving more milestones. With curiosity, perseverance, and a positive attitude, I believe that the possibilities are endless.

To my fellow learners: **Find joy in learning, keep asking questions, and always believe in yourself. The world is full of opportunities waiting to be explored!**

# 75

# RITVIK CHOUDHARY

# Chasing Dreams: My Journey into Acting

### The Spark of Passion

Hi, I'm Ritvik Choudhary, a Grade 7 learner at 21K School, and acting has been my passion for as long as I can remember. From a young age, I was drawn to films, theater, and storytelling, and I knew I wanted to be part of this world. However, my journey has not been without challenges - rejections, waiting, and balancing academics with auditions have all tested my resilience.

### The Reality of Pursuing Acting

Stepping into the world of acting has been both exciting and unpredictable. I have auditioned for multiple projects, some of which seemed promising, only to fall through. Despite this, I never let disappointment define me. Every experience taught me something new - whether about expressing emotions, understanding characters, or staying patient in an industry that requires perseverance.

### Overcoming Challenges

Balancing my studies and acting career has been one of my biggest hurdles. There were days when I had to prepare for an exam while memorizing lines for a role. However, I was lucky to have supportive friends and family who helped me stay on track.

21K School played an instrumental role in making this balance possible. The flexible schedule and online learning environment allowed me to focus on acting without compromising my education.

Participating in school events and skits also helped me hone my confidence and stage presence.

## Learning Beyond the Screen

Through acting, I have learned skills that extend beyond performance:

- Emotional intelligence: Understanding different characters has helped me connect with people on a deeper level.

- Patience and resilience: Rejections no longer discourage me - they push me to improve.

- Confidence: I've learned to step out of my comfort zone, embrace challenges, and believe in myself.

## Looking to the Future

As I continue on this journey, I am excited for the opportunities that lie ahead. Acting is more than just a dream for me - it's my calling. I know that every role, every audition, and every challenge is shaping me into the artist I aspire to be.

To my fellow learners: **Follow your passion, stay patient, and keep improving. Every setback is just a stepping stone toward your dream!**

# 76

## RIZWIN FAROOK

# Smashing Boundaries: The Road to Badminton Glory

**My Love for the Game**

Hi, I'm Rizwin Farook, a dedicated badminton player, and my journey has been defined by grit, discipline, and perseverance. From the moment I first picked up a badminton racket, I knew this sport would be an integral part of my life. Over the years, my passion has led me to win seven trophies, each representing countless hours of practice and sacrifice.

Achievements That Keep Me Motivated

Among my proudest achievements are:

- Three first-place victories in inter-academy tournaments at Al Masah Academy.
- Reaching the semifinals at the Ranking Gold Junior Tournament at Xtra Sharjah.
- Advancing to the quarterfinals at Prime Star Dubai.
- Securing the runner-up position in the Men's Doubles D category at SBA Sharjah.
- Receiving the 'Emerging Player' award at Al Masah Academy.
- These moments have shaped my confidence, proving that dedication and persistence always pay off.

**Overcoming Challenges**

The path to success hasn't been easy. Long training hours, fatigue, and sacrifices were all part of the journey.

Sometimes, I had to miss social gatherings, cut back on leisure activities, and push through physical exhaustion. Losing matches was especially tough, but I learned that setbacks are not failures - they are lessons in resilience.

Each loss only fueled my desire to come back stronger. I trained harder, worked on my weaknesses, and learned the importance of mental toughness. Badminton has taught me that consistency, not just talent, is the key to success.

## The Role of 21K School

Balancing academics with competitive sports is a challenge, but 21K School's flexible learning system has made it possible. With the ability to study at my own pace, I can dedicate sufficient time to both education and training without feeling overwhelmed.

## Looking to the Future

Badminton is not just a sport for me - it's a way of life. My next goal is to compete in international tournaments and represent my country on the global stage. I am committed to working harder, improving my skills, and proving that dedication can turn dreams into reality.

To my fellow learners: **Never be afraid to chase your dreams. Challenges will come, but every challenge is an opportunity to grow. Keep pushing, keep training, and success will follow!**

# 77

# Ryan Anish

# Strumming the Strings of Success: A Journey in Music

## A Passion That Started Early

Hi, I'm Ryan Anish, a Grade 5 learner from Bangalore, India, currently studying under the British Pathway at 21K School. My journey into music started at the age of three, when I first saw a band perform. While most people admired the overall music, I was captivated by the guitarist, watching the way they moved their fingers and created melodies. That moment sparked something in me, and I knew I wanted to learn the guitar.

## The Challenges of Learning Music

Learning the guitar wasn't easy. Initially, I struggled to balance school, practice sessions, and my daily routine. My first attempt at the Trinity Guitar exam didn't go as planned, and I felt disappointed. However, my parents and teachers encouraged me, reminding me that every mistake was a lesson in disguise. Their support helped me push forward and develop my skills with renewed determination.

## Achievements That Define Me

One of my proudest moments was receiving a Trinity Guitar distinction, an honor only four learners in my class achieved. This milestone was not just about passing an exam - it was a testament to my perseverance, hours of practice, and belief in myself.

### The Role of 21K School

A turning point in my journey was joining 21K School. The flexible learning schedule allowed me to dedicate more time to music without compromising my academics. I started practicing daily, experimenting with new sounds, and developing my own techniques to refine my skills.

### Looking to the Future

My dream is to pass all eight Trinity School grades for guitar and continue honing my craft. This journey has taught me that practice makes perfect, and mistakes are stepping stones to success.

To my fellow learners: **Never give up. Celebrate your mistakes, for they are your greatest teachers. Keep working hard, and you'll achieve your dreams!**

# 78

# SAHANA T. M.

# Melodies of Resilience: A Journey Through Music

## The Power of Music

Hi, I'm Sahana T. M., a dedicated learner at 21K School from Bangalore, India. Music has always been more than just an art form for me - it is my passion, solace, and a way of healing. My journey in Carnatic vocal music began at the age of five, inspired by my parents' dream of seeing me shine in the world of music.

## Finding My Voice in Carnatic Music

From a young age, I trained under my guru, Ms. Lavanya Rupakula, who nurtured my love for Carnatic music. Under her guidance, I learned to appreciate the rich history and intricate details of classical compositions. As I progressed, I expanded my musical knowledge by learning the keyboard, which helped me understand music theory, composition, and rhythm.

## Overcoming Life's Greatest Challenge

Despite my deep passion for music, my journey took an unexpected turn when I was diagnosed with a terminal brain illness. This became the biggest test of my resilience and determination. Instead of letting it hold me back, I used music as a source of strength. I continued composing, blending Carnatic music with fusion elements, and experimenting with different instruments. One of my proudest moments was adapting India's National Anthem into a Carnatic rendition, which earned recognition from PRISM JOHNSON PVT LTD, Mumbai, and the title of India's Talented Kid.

## Achievements That Inspire Me

Some of my key accomplishments include:

Earning the title of "Sangeeta Kuyil" from a renowned Chennai temple for my Carnatic skills.

Being featured in a local newspaper for my contributions to music.

Participating in multiple music concerts, spreading joy through my voice.

## The Role of 21K School

21K School has been a beacon of support in my journey. The flexible learning environment allowed me to focus on both my music and my academics. My teachers, especially Ms. Charu Jethwani and Ms. Ishita Roy Chowdhury, played a crucial role in refining my writing and musical expression.

## Looking to the Future

Music has been my guiding light, helping me navigate even the most difficult times. My goal is to keep evolving as a musician, explore new techniques, and inspire others through my art.

To my fellow learners: **Every challenge is an opportunity to grow. Stay committed, stay positive, and believe in yourself. Music has the power to heal, inspire, and transform lives!**

# 79

# Shambavi S Bhatt

# The Mind of a Writer

## Discovering My Passion

I've always loved stories. From a young age, I found myself drawn to books, fascinated by the way words created entire worlds. As I grew older, I realized I didn't just want to read stories - I wanted to write them. Writing became my way of expressing emotions, ideas, and dreams.

## Achievements That Define Me

- Won first place in a national creative writing competition.
- Published multiple short stories in school magazines.
- Started my own blog, sharing my thoughts and creative pieces.

## Overcoming Challenges

Writing wasn't always easy. There were times when I doubted myself, wondering if my words were good enough. I struggled with structuring my stories and finding the right words. But with perseverance, feedback from mentors, and constant practice, I refined my skills and became more confident in my abilities.

## The Role of 21K School

21K School provided me with the encouragement I needed to continue my journey as a writer. My teachers and peers celebrated my successes and helped me grow by providing constructive criticism.

The flexible learning environment allowed me to dedicate more time to writing while balancing my academics.

## Looking to the Future

My dream is to become a published author, inspiring others through my words. I believe stories have the power to change perspectives, and I want to contribute to the world through storytelling.

To my fellow learners: **"Your words matter. Keep writing, keep creating, and never be afraid to share your story."**

# 80

## SHANMUKHA MIHIRA

# Dancing with Passion

### Finding My Rhythm

Ever since I was a toddler, I've loved dancing. Music speaks to me in a way that words sometimes cannot. I feel the rhythm, the beats, and my body moves instinctively. Bharatanatyam, in particular, has been a significant part of my journey, helping me connect with my culture and express emotions through movement.

### Achievements That Define Me

- Performed at multiple cultural events and competitions.

- Received awards for excellence in Bharatanatyam.

- Choreographed and performed original dance sequences.

### Overcoming Challenges

Dancing requires immense discipline, practice, and stamina. There were times when I felt exhausted, struggling to perfect my moves. But I learned that persistence and passion can overcome any obstacle. The support of my dance mentors and my family kept me going.

### The Role of 21K School

21K School allowed me to pursue my passion while keeping up with my studies. The flexibility in scheduling meant I could attend my dance rehearsals and competitions without falling behind in academics.

## Looking to the Future

I dream of becoming a professional dancer and sharing my love for Bharatanatyam with the world. Dance is not just an art - it's a language of the soul.

To my fellow learners: **"Follow your passion fearlessly. Dance like nobody's watching, and live like every step tells a story."**

# 81

## SHAURYA DAVID

# Stepping into My Potential: A Journey of Growth & Excellence

**The Path to Discovery**

Hi, I'm Shaurya David, a Grade 7 learner in the British Pathway at 21K School, from Gurugram, India. My journey has been a blend of curiosity, learning, and pushing my limits in both academics and extracurriculars. With a passion for reading that fuels my imagination and a love for cricket that keeps me energized, I have learned the importance of balance, perseverance, and continuous growth.

**Celebrating Milestones**

This year has been especially rewarding for me. Some of my biggest achievements include:

Being named Star Performer for Term 1 in Class 7MD.

Winning the Star Performer title on Day 1 of the Lit Fest after delivering a speech that helped me overcome my stage fright.

Receiving a certificate for 100% attendance in June, showcasing my dedication to learning.

Each milestone has strengthened my belief that consistent effort and active participation lead to excellence.

**Overcoming Challenges**

Balancing academics with extracurricular commitments hasn't always been easy. Preparing for the Lit Fest while keeping up with schoolwork was a challenge.

Overcoming my initial fear of public speaking felt daunting, but I learned that preparation and persistence can turn any fear into confidence. These experiences helped me develop better time management and organization skills.

## The Role of 21K School

21K School has been an incredible support system. The personalized learning environment and encouragement from facilitators have helped me explore my potential beyond textbooks. The Lit Fest became a turning point, allowing me to develop public speaking skills and express my thoughts with clarity and confidence.

## Looking to the Future

My dream is to pursue a career in robotics and technology. The idea of creating innovations that can make a difference in the world excites me. With the right mindset and support, I believe I can achieve my goals.

To my fellow learners: **Believe in yourself, embrace challenges, and trust the journey. Every small step you take brings you closer to success!**

# 82

## SHOBHIT MALEKAR

# Beyond the Surface: Redefining Strength and Leadership

### A Different Perspective on Disability

Hi, I'm Shobhit Malekar, born in 2007 with Charcot-Marie-Tooth (CMT), a rare genetic condition that affects my ability to move my hands and feet easily. But I have never let this define me. Instead of seeing disability as a limitation, I have come to understand that true strength lies in resilience, adaptability, and perspective.

### The Power of Perspective

For a long time, I questioned the label of "disabled." I realized that many people, despite being physically capable, struggle with managing their thoughts, emotions, and relationships. Observing this made me redefine disability - not just as a physical condition but as an inability to adapt, grow, or find purpose. This perspective has shaped my approach to leadership and self-growth.

### Leading with Purpose

Rather than focusing on what I cannot do, I have focused on what I can do:

- As the school president, I work towards creating an inclusive environment where every learner feels valued.

- I have embraced my role as a mentor, guiding and encouraging others to believe in themselves.

- I have learned that true leadership is about empowering people and turning challenges into opportunities.

## Overcoming Challenges

There have been moments of self-doubt and pressure, but my journey has taught me the power of perseverance and gratitude. With the support of my family, friends, and mentors, I have developed a positive mindset that helps me navigate struggles and focus on progress.

## The Role of 21K School

21K School has given me the freedom to grow beyond limitations. The flexible learning model and mentorship provided by the school have allowed me to develop skills in leadership, communication, and self-awareness.

## Looking to the Future

I am committed to making a positive impact by challenging stereotypes around disability and promoting inclusivity and growth. My goal is to help others see their potential, regardless of the challenges they face.

To my fellow learners: **You are stronger than you think. With determination and self-belief, you can achieve anything. Embrace your journey and redefine success on your own terms!**

# 83

SHOUNAK R SUVARNA

# Chasing the Dream: Tennis, Triumphs & the Power

## The Road to the Top

Hi, I'm Shounak Suvarna, a Grade 9 learner from Kolhapur, Maharashtra, currently training in Nice, France, to pursue my dream of becoming a professional tennis player. Tennis has been my lifelong passion, and I have dedicated years of training and perseverance to compete at national and international levels.

## Achievements That Define Me

My journey in tennis has been filled with exciting milestones:

- Ranked No. 4 in India in the Under-12 and Under-14 categories.
- Ranked No. 25 in all of Asia in the Under-14 category.
- Winner of 13 national tournaments in the Under-12 category and 16 in the Under-14 category.
- Champion in three Asian tournaments in the Under-14 category.
- Winner of two Under-16 French national tournaments.
- Currently competing in International Tennis Federation (ITF) tournaments worldwide.

## Overcoming Challenges

Despite my passion and success, my journey has not been without struggles. Managing a rigorous training schedule - which involves six hours of daily practice - alongside academics, family, and social life has been a major challenge.

Living away from home for most of the year is another sacrifice I have had to make, but I stay motivated by keeping my eyes on my goal.

## The Role of 21K School

21K School has played a crucial role in balancing my education and sports career. With time zone differences making it difficult to attend live classes, I rely on recorded lessons and flexible exam schedules to stay on track. The support from facilitators has allowed me to focus on my training without compromising my academics.

## Looking to the Future

My dream is to turn professional within the next two years and achieve success in ITF tournaments. I know that every challenge I face today is preparing me for an even bigger future in tennis.

To my fellow learners: **Dream big, protect your dream, and never let anyone tell you it's impossible. Anything is achievable with passion and perseverance!**

# 84

## SOHAM NAIK

# Kicks, Cuts, and Comebacks: My Taekwondo Tale

## A Fighter's Journey

Hi, I'm Soham Naik, a passionate taekwondo athlete from Pune, Maharashtra. My journey in martial arts began in 2022, and since then, I have faced and conquered challenges that have shaped me into the determined athlete I am today.

## Early Success and Challenges

When I first stepped onto the taekwondo mat, I had no idea how much this sport would change me. Just six months into training, I competed in the Pune Taekwondo Festival and won a bronze medal. This victory fueled my hunger for more.

However, my journey was not always smooth. My second tournament at the 3rd Pune District Championship ended in disappointment, as I failed to secure a medal. Instead of giving up, I vowed to train harder.

## The Injury That Tested Me

Just when I was preparing for my next tournament, I faced a major setback - an injury to my right toe that left me unable to walk for 15 days. Doctors advised me to rest for a month, and I worried about falling behind in training. Once I recovered, I struggled to regain my speed, strength, and confidence, but I refused to let this setback define me.

## Bouncing Back Stronger

Determined to prove myself, I pushed through intense training sessions, focusing on my technique, endurance, and mental strength. At my next district-level championship, I won:

- Silver in kyorugi (fights).
- Gold and silver in poomsae (forms).

Winning at the district level earned me a spot at the Maharashtra State Taekwondo Championship. Competing at the state level was a whole new experience, as I faced elite athletes with exceptional skills. I was nervous but focused. When I won a bronze medal, I felt an immense sense of achievement.

## The Role of 21K School

21K School has been instrumental in my academic and athletic balance. The flexible learning model allows me to dedicate adequate time to training while staying on top of my studies.

Looking to the Future

With my blue belt in taekwondo, I am more determined than ever to push my limits, compete at the highest levels, and earn my black belt. Taekwondo has taught me that every setback is a setup for a greater comeback.

To my fellow learners: **Hard work, resilience, and perseverance will take you further than talent alone. Stay focused, stay determined, and success will follow!**

# 85

# SRIKRUTHI DUMPALA

# Mastering the Mental Game: My Tennis Journey

## Chasing Dreams on the Court

Hi, I'm Srikruthi Dumpala, a passionate tennis player from Telangana, India. Tennis has been an integral part of my life for as long as I can remember. Today, I am ranked 44 by the All India Tennis Association and 344 in the Under-14 category, but my journey to this point has been anything but easy.

## Learning to Overcome Mental Barriers

Tennis is not just about skill - it's about mental strength. Early in my career, I struggled with controlling my emotions on the court. Whether it was frustration from losing a point or excitement from being ahead, my emotions often affected my performance. This led to moments where I lost matches that I should have won simply because I let my emotions get the better of me.

The turning point came when I asked myself: Was I afraid of losing, or was I putting too much pressure on winning? I realized that success wasn't about always leading - it was about staying composed even when behind. I started practicing deep breathing, mental focus, and visualization techniques, which slowly helped me regain control of my emotions.

## The Role of 21K School

Before joining 21K School, balancing tennis and academics was a struggle. I often had to miss classes for tournaments, and my grades suffered.

21K School's flexible learning model allowed me to attend classes at my own pace and watch recorded lessons whenever I missed a session. This approach transformed my education without forcing me to choose between sports and studies.

## Looking to the Future

My journey has taught me that success is not just about talent - it's about mental resilience and consistent effort. Every setback is an opportunity to grow. I aspire to continue improving my ranking and competing at international tournaments, knowing that I have the skills and mindset to succeed.

To my fellow learners: **Follow your passion, trust the process, and never let fear hold you back. The court - like life - rewards those who persevere!**

# Flipping Towards Success: My Journey in Gymnastics

## A Leap of Faith

Hi, I'm Srisha Sethi, a Grade 2 learner from Suratgarh, Rajasthan, and my journey is filled with dance, drama, skating, badminton, and gymnastics. While I love all these activities, my heart truly belongs to gymnastics, where I've learned the power of discipline, perseverance, and self-belief.

## Small Steps to Big Achievements

Gymnastics isn't easy. When I first started, even the simplest moves felt impossible - balancing on the beam, perfecting rolls, or learning flips. But I never gave up. I set small goals and focused on improving one step at a time. My parents and coach were always there to cheer me on, reminding me that progress matters more than perfection.

Competing in my first in-house gymnastics competition was nerve-wracking but exciting. After months of preparation, I performed cartwheels, handstands, and a flawless beam routine. Winning a gold medal for beam, silver as an all-rounder, and bronze in the floor routine was an unforgettable moment!

## The Role of 21K School

21K School has helped me build confidence and balance academics with my passion. Through events like Sports Day and creative learning methods, I've learned to embrace challenges and enjoy every step of my journey.

## Looking to the Future

I dream of combining my love for gymnastics with my passion for performing arts. Whether I become an athlete or a performer, I know that persistence and self-belief will take me far.

To my fellow learners: **Never be afraid to take the first step. Growth happens when you step out of your comfort zone, and every challenge shapes you into the best version of yourself!**

# 87

## STUTHI S. SHETTY

# Chasing Excellence: A Journey of Dedication

### The Power of Passion and Hard Work

Hi, I'm Stuthi S. Shetty, a Grade 5 learner at 21K School in Bangalore, Karnataka. My journey has been a combination of sports, academics, and resilience. I have a deep passion for badminton and squash, but I also love reading and learning new things. Balancing all my interests has been a challenge, but it has taught me valuable life lessons.

### Achievements That Inspire Me

My hard work has led me to achieve some incredible milestones:

- Silver medal in the Karnataka State Ranking Tournament at Selenite Badminton Academy, Bangalore.

- Silver at DYES Badminton Academy.

- Gold at the Karnataka State Ranking Tournament in Chikmagalur, making me the Under-11 Karnataka State Champion.

- Reached the Nationals, ranked among the top 8 in India, and won silver in the doubles category.

### Overcoming Challenges

Balancing school and intense training has been difficult. I have faced physical challenges, including injuries that tested my endurance. But instead of giving up, I created a timetable to balance both academics and sports, ensuring I never fall behind in either.

## The Role of 21K School

21K School has played a crucial role in my growth. With flexible learning, ATL, and HOM programs, I developed better study habits and confidence. The school's Literary Fest, Mathalon, and GK Quiz helped enhance my skills beyond the sports arena.

## Looking to the Future

I dream of becoming an Olympic Gold Medalist in badminton, and I am determined to give my best in both academics and sports.

To my fellow learners: **Success isn't about shortcuts - it's about resilience, persistence, and passion. Keep pushing forward!**

# MOHAMMAD SULEMAAN HAADI

# From Numbers to Marathons: My Growth and Achievement

## A Journey of Exploration and Excellence

Hi, I'm Mohammad Sulemaan Haadi, a Grade 3 learner at 21K School, from Kolkata, India. My journey is filled with science, football, taekwondo, reading, and long-distance running. I love pushing my limits and discovering new challenges every day.

## Achievements That Keep Me Motivated

- Proud Global Awardee at the Global Kids Achievers Awards.
- Gold Medalist in the World Maths Championship.
- Green Stripe Yellow Belt in Taekwondo at the United Amateur Taekwondo Academy.
- Completed a 10 km run at the TCS Fit4Life Corporate Challenge.
- Participated in the 5 km Kolkata Police Safe Drive Save Life Marathon twice.

## Overcoming Challenges

Managing academics, sports, and competitive exams is demanding, but I have learned time management and consistency. My family and mentors have been my biggest support system.

## Looking Ahead

I aim to continue excelling in academics and athletics, proving that with determination and perseverance, anything is possible.

To my fellow learners: **Success is a journey, not just a destination. Stay committed and keep pushing forward!**

# Surlaksh Shaanvi

# Dancing Through Life: A Journey of Passion & Resilience

## A World of Creativity and Movement

Hi, I'm Surlaksh Shaanvi, a Grade 2 learner at 21K School, living in the beautiful state of West Bengal, India. My journey has been filled with dance, gymnastics, badminton, hip-hop, B-boying, and Abacus, but the most special part of it is my love for Kathak dance. Each day brings a new opportunity to explore, learn, and grow.

## Achievements That Inspire Me

Over time, I've built a strong foundation in both academics and extracurriculars. Some of my proudest achievements include:

- Bronze medal in the North Bengal Cultural Competitions in both 2024 and 2025.

- Prodigy Award at the MAA International Online Abacus Championship 2024.

- A medal and certificate at the All India Talent Search Examination.

- 3rd place in a solo Kathak dance competition in January 2025.

One of my biggest learnings came from my Kathak competition. In the middle of my performance, I forgot one step. But instead of panicking, I remained calm, held my posture, and found my way back into the rhythm. That moment taught me the importance of grace under pressure, and I was proud of my ability to adapt and keep going.

## Overcoming Challenges

Balancing schoolwork with my many interests was not always easy. There were times when I felt nervous before performing, and I struggled with managing my time between practice, school, and personal hobbies. However, with structured planning, perseverance, and encouragement from my parents and teachers, I learned that hard work and patience always lead to success.

## The Role of 21K School

21K School has played a huge role in shaping my confidence and skills. The flexible schedule allows me to train and compete without feeling overwhelmed. My teachers have always been encouraging, providing guidance in both academics and extracurriculars.

## Looking Ahead

I dream of winning gold medals in dance competitions and excelling in all my chosen fields. With dedication and hard work, I know that no dream is too big!

To my fellow learners: **Stay passionate, embrace challenges, and always believe in yourself. Every setback is a step closer to success!**

# 90

# Swaraj Mishra

# Checkmate to Success: My Journey in Chess

## Discovering My Passion for Chess

Hi, I'm Swaraj Mishra, a Grade 3 learner from Pune, Maharashtra, India. I have always loved science, technology, and solving tricky math problems, but my biggest passion is chess. The thrill of planning moves, outsmarting my opponent, and thinking two steps ahead is what makes the game so exciting.

## Achievements That Define Me

One of my proudest moments was winning a gold medal in my first chess tournament. It was a tough competition, and I was nervous at first. But I reminded myself of the lessons my teachers and parents taught me - never give up and always try my best. As the matches progressed, my confidence grew, and when I finally won, I felt an incredible sense of accomplishment.

## Overcoming Challenges

Chess isn't just about making moves; it's about staying calm and focused when things don't go as planned. At times, I made mistakes that cost me games, and I felt frustrated. Balancing school and daily chess practice was also a challenge. However, I learned to create a study schedule, set small goals, and stay disciplined in my approach. Over time, my gameplay improved, and I became a better strategist.

## The Role of 21K School

21K School has been a great support in my journey. My teachers encourage me to explore new things, push my limits, and never give up. Participating in Olympiads and interactive learning challenges has helped me develop problem-solving skills that are useful both in chess and in life.

## Looking to the Future

I dream of becoming a Grandmaster in chess and competing in international tournaments. I know that it will take years of dedication, patience, and continuous learning, but I am ready for the challenge!

To my fellow learners: **Never fear big dreams. If you work hard and believe in yourself, anything is possible!**

# 91

## SYED JUNAID BASHEER

# A Journey of Numbers and Goals

### My Love for Numbers

Hi, I'm Syed Junaid Basheer, a Grade 5 learner in British 5MB at 21K School, living in Jizan, Saudi Arabia. My journey is one filled with challenges, discoveries, and personal growth, especially in the field of Abacus, math, and analytical thinking. Apart from numbers, I also love solving cubes, playing football, cycling, and swimming.

### Achievements That Define Me

My journey with Abacus began in 2020 when I was just seven years old. What started as a way to improve my calculation skills soon became a passion. One of my proudest moments was securing 1st rank at the Intermediate level of Abacus, a testament to my dedication and practice.

### Overcoming Challenges

When I first started learning Abacus, I faced nervousness and time management issues. I often doubted myself, wondering if I could ever reach the speed and accuracy needed to compete at a higher level. However, through daily practice and persistence, I improved my abilities and developed confidence in problem-solving.

My journey was never a solo effort - my parents and teachers played a vital role. Their unwavering belief in me kept me motivated, even when I felt like giving up. Their encouragement helped me realize that hard work and dedication can turn any dream into reality.

## The Role of 21K School

Being a part of 21K School has been an incredible advantage. The personalized learning system and flexibility allowed me to train for Abacus competitions while excelling in academics. The support from my teachers and peers has pushed me to keep challenging myself.

## Looking Ahead

My journey with numbers is just beginning. I dream of competing at international Abacus championships and using my analytical skills in fields like technology, science, and engineering.

To my fellow learners: **Numbers are more than just calculations; they are a language of possibilities. Stay curious, practice hard, and success will follow!**

# 92

## TEJAS

# Turning Dreams into Reality

## My Passion for Learning and Innovation

Hi, I'm Tejas, an 11th-grade learner at 21K School, following the British Curriculum. From the moment I joined, I had big aspirations - to excel in academics, dive into technology, and gain real-world experience. Today, I am proud to say that 21K School has helped me achieve all of this and more.

## Achievements That Define Me

One of my proudest accomplishments is securing A grades in five IGCSE subjects*, but my journey extends beyond academics. I have had the opportunity to enter the professional world while still in school, working as:

- A Software Developer at Antern.

- The Lead Backend Developer at Second Brain Labs, where I built a backend system for customer support analysis.

Knowing that my code is used in real-world applications daily has been an incredibly fulfilling experience.

## Overcoming Challenges

Balancing academics with professional work was no easy feat. There were days when I had to prepare for exams while debugging code, managing both deadlines and school assignments simultaneously. At times, it felt overwhelming, but I learned to prioritize, stay disciplined, and manage time efficiently.

## The Role of 21K School

21K School's flexible learning structure was a game-changer. The freedom to schedule classes around my work commitments allowed me to pursue my passion without compromising academics. The support from my teachers in Mathematics, Physics, Chemistry, and ICT ensured that I could grasp complex concepts even when working under pressure.

One of my most memorable experiences was meeting Ronnie Screwvala, a visionary entrepreneur, who inspired me to keep pushing forward in my tech journey.

## Looking to the Future

While I continue my A and AS level studies, my ambitions go beyond just academics. I aim to launch startups that solve real-world problems, combining my technical expertise with innovation.

To my fellow learners: **Dream big, stay committed, and embrace challenges. The path to success isn't always easy, but with the right mindset and support, anything is possible!**

# 93

# TEJASHWINI MAHENDRAN

# Smashing Limits: My Journey in Badminton and Beyond

## A Passion for the Game

Hi, I'm Tejashwini Mahendran, a Grade 12 learner and a national-level badminton player from Hyderabad, India. My life revolves around balancing two major passions: badminton and academics. This balancing act has shaped me into a disciplined and focused individual, always striving to break new limits.

## Achievements That Define Me

I have dedicated years to badminton, competing at district, state, and national-level tournaments. Some of my key achievements include:

- Winning multiple state-level championships.

- Representing my state in national badminton tournaments.

- Training rigorously to improve my technique and endurance.

## Overcoming Challenges

Balancing intense training schedules with academics has often felt overwhelming. There were moments when I doubted my ability to succeed in both fields. However, instead of giving up, these challenges fueled my drive to work harder.

## The Role of 21K School

21K School's flexible schedules and personalized lesson plans allowed me to stay on top of my studies while pursuing my sporting goals.

The mentorship I received helped build my time management skills and boosted my confidence.

## Looking Ahead

I aspire to represent India in international badminton tournaments and pursue a career in sports science. My journey has taught me that success isn't solely about talent - it's about resilience, discipline, and the right support system.

To my fellow learners: **Never give up on your dreams. With determination, resilience, and the right support, anything is possible!**

# THRISHAN KUMAR M

# The Journey of a Badminton Player

## The Love for Badminton

Hi, I'm Thrishan Kumar M, a Grade 9 learner from Bangalore, India. Badminton isn't just a sport for me - it's my passion and purpose. Over the years, I've achieved milestones that have pushed me closer to my dream of representing India in the Olympics.

## Achievements That Inspire Me

- Ranked 3rd in Karnataka in the Under-15 singles category.

- Ranked 29th in India in Under-15 badminton.

- Winner of two bronze medals in doubles at the state level.

## Overcoming Challenges

Balancing academics with a rigorous training schedule was a challenge. Before 21K School, attending a traditional school while dedicating hours to badminton felt impossible. With 21K's flexible learning structure, I could focus on my sport without compromising my education.

## Looking to the Future

My ultimate goal is to represent India in the Olympics. I know it will take years of perseverance and hard work, but I am committed to making it happen.

To my fellow learners: **Never give up on your dreams, no matter how tough the road gets. Keep pushing forward!**

# Vaidic Mukherjee

# Chasing Stars and Dreams

## The Power of Curiosity

Hi, I'm Vaidic Mukherjee, a Grade 4 learner at 21K School in New Delhi, India. My world is filled with exploration, creativity, and a hunger to learn new things. Whether it's stargazing, karate, playing the keyboard, building Lego models, or solving Rubik's cubes, I believe that every activity adds something unique to my journey. My motto in life is inspired by Swami Vivekananda's words: "All power is within you; you can do anything and everything."

## Achievements That Inspire Me

My journey has been shaped by my love for karate, space, writing, and cricket. Some of my key achievements include:

- Winning multiple medals in the World Karate Federation (WKF) tournaments and securing a senior-most brown belt.

- Participating in the Delhi Olympics 2024 and securing fourth place.

- Winning the All India Space Quiz organized by the Ministry of Culture, a milestone that fueled my love for astronomy.

- Becoming an award-winning author after publishing my book The Land of Goomba.

- Meeting cricket legends Chris Gayle and Irfan Pathan during the Legends League Cricket in Kashmir and getting featured on Star Sports.

## Overcoming Challenges

Every journey comes with challenges, and mine has been no different. My first karate championship at the age of 7 was nerve-wracking, especially when I had to face international competitors. I managed to win a bronze medal, proving to myself that fear can be conquered with preparation and perseverance.

Balancing my multiple passions with academics has also been a challenge. There were times when I felt overwhelmed with my commitments, but I have learned to manage my time effectively, ensuring that I give my best to everything I love.

## The Role of 21K School

21K School has been my second family. The flexibility of online learning has allowed me to pursue my interests without compromising on education. Programs like astronomy coaching, the Lit Fest, and Republic Day celebrations have boosted my confidence and broadened my knowledge.

## Looking to the Future

I dream of working with ISRO or NASA as a space scientist and achieving the 10th DAN black belt in karate. I also plan to explore coding and robotics, adding new dimensions to my learning journey.

To my fellow learners: **"Choose your favorite activity and make it your passion. Never stop exploring, learning, and believing in yourself."**

# VIR CHATTUR

# A Champion's Court: A Journey of Grit and Goals

## The Heart of a Tennis Player

Hi, I'm Vir Chattur, a Grade 6 learner at 21K School, based in Pune, India. My journey in tennis has been one of perseverance, discipline, and determination. Ranked 8th nationally in the U-12 boys' category, I have dedicated myself to excelling in this sport while maintaining my academic growth.

## Achievements That Define Me

Tennis has taken me across India and Asia, competing against some of the best young athletes. Some of my proudest achievements include:

- Runner-up in the Maharashtra U-12 Masters tournament.

- Training rigorously for five hours daily, pushing my limits every single day.

- Competing in national and international tournaments, learning to adapt to different playing conditions and surfaces.

## Overcoming Challenges

Balancing academics and an intense training schedule has been my biggest challenge. With five hours of practice each day and frequent travel for tournaments, I have had to learn time management, discipline, and resilience. Some days, exhaustion sets in, but my passion for tennis and my dream of playing professionally keep me motivated.

## The Role of 21K School

21K School has been my biggest support system, offering flexible learning that allows me to study from anywhere - whether at a tournament venue or a hotel room. Recorded classes have been a lifesaver, and my teachers have always been there to help me catch up and stay on track academically.

## Looking to the Future

I dream of representing India on the international tennis stage and competing in Grand Slam tournaments. My goal is to inspire other young athletes to chase their dreams with dedication and resilience.

To my fellow learners: **"Dream big, work hard, and never let challenges stop you. Every match, every practice session, and every late-night study session is a step towards your goal!"**

# 97

# VISMMAYA

# Grace and Strength: My Journey in Yoga and Bharatanatyam

**The Beginning of a Passion**

Hi, I'm Vismmaya, a Grade 1 learner from Palani, Tamil Nadu. At just six years old, I have discovered my love for yoga and Bharatanatyam, two ancient Indian traditions that have shaped me into the person I am today. What started as a simple activity to improve my daily routine has now become my greatest passion.

**Achievements That Inspire Me**

From the age of 2.5 years, I have dedicated myself to yoga and dance, and my journey has led to incredible achievements:

- Three world records in yoga at the age of four, including holding the Poorna Bhujangasana (Full Cobra Pose) for 10 minutes.

- Completing 108 Surya Namaskars (Sun Salutations), a testament to my strength and endurance.

- Winning silver and gold medals at the International Yoga Championship in Sri Lanka.

- Earning a silver medal at the 1st Asian Yoga Championship in Sri Lanka in 2024.

- Performing at the prestigious Natiyanjali Festival at Palani, Rameswaram, and Thiruvarur temples, receiving the title of Natyatharakai.

## Overcoming Challenges

Every success comes with challenges. Holding difficult yoga poses for extended periods required discipline, patience, and intense practice. At times, my muscles ached, and I felt like giving up, but my love for yoga kept me going. Similarly, learning the intricate movements of Bharatanatyam took hours of dedication and repetition, but with perseverance, I improved day by day.

## The Role of 21K School

21K School has been a strong pillar in my journey, allowing me to balance my education with my passions. With a flexible learning structure, I can practice and compete without falling behind in my studies.

## Looking Ahead

I dream of continuing my journey in yoga and Bharatanatyam, inspiring others to embrace these art forms. My goal is to represent India on international platforms and encourage young learners to believe in themselves.

To my fellow learners: **"No dream is too big when you have passion and dedication. Keep practicing, keep believing, and success will follow!"**

# 98

## Vivaan Rao

# Rising Above: A Journey of Commitment and Growth

### Defining My Path

Hi, I'm Vivaan Rao, an 11-year-old Grade 5 learner at 21K School in Bangalore, India. I have always been passionate about reading, badminton, and exploring new knowledge. This year has been a journey of learning, perseverance, and pushing beyond my limits.

### Achievements That Define Me

This year, I reached milestones that reinforced my belief in hard work and dedication:

- Achieved 100% attendance for the entire term, proving my commitment to consistency and discipline.

- Actively participated in the Inter House GK Quiz, demonstrating my love for knowledge and competition.

- Balanced academics with extracurricular activities, making sure I excel in both.

### Overcoming Challenges

One of the biggest challenges I faced was finding balance between studies and personal interests. There were times when distractions made it difficult to focus. However, I realized that self-discipline and time management were the keys to success. My parents and teachers played a crucial role in guiding me back on track whenever I felt lost.

## The Role of 21K School

21K School has transformed my learning experience. The Century Tech tools introduced this year provided me with personalized learning resources, helping me identify and work on my strengths and weaknesses. My teachers, especially Ramya Ma'am, have been instrumental in keeping me motivated and focused on my goals.

## Looking to the Future

I have learned that every challenge is an opportunity to grow. My goal is to continue striving for excellence in academics and sports while developing critical thinking and leadership skills.

To my fellow learners: **"Every step you take, no matter how small, brings you closer to your dreams. Stay committed, stay curious, and never stop learning!"**

# 99

## VIYAAN ARORA

# Turning Imagination into Reality

### A Mind Full of Ideas

Hi, I'm Viyaan Arora, a Grade 2 learner from New Delhi, India. From an early age, I have been fascinated by stories, science, and creativity. Whether it's writing books, painting, or excelling in academics, I believe that curiosity and passion can take us anywhere.

### Achievements That Define Me

My journey has been full of exciting accomplishments:

- Published four books, two of which - Magical Castle and Adventures of Dilly and Villy - have ISBN recognition from the Ministry of Education.

- Won the Best Seller Trophy at the National Young Author's Fair in 2023.

- Secured a Gold Medal in NSTSE with an international rank of 12.

- Won Silver in ISTSE Summer and Gold Medals in English and Mathematics Olympiads.

### Overcoming Challenges

While I have always been passionate about learning, I used to struggle with completing assignments independently, speaking fluently in English, and maintaining neat work. Through dedicated practice and support from my teachers, I have improved my confidence and skills, making learning an enjoyable experience.

## The Role of 21K School

21K School has played a crucial role in developing my creative and academic abilities. Programs like ATL and HOM have helped me think critically and explore new ideas, while events such as the Literary Fest, Mathalon, and Science Fest have provided opportunities to showcase my talents.

## Looking to the Future

I dream of becoming a scientist or an artist, using my creativity to make a difference. My journey has taught me that challenges are just stepping stones to success.

To my fellow learners: **"Never give up on your dreams. Every challenge you overcome makes you stronger and takes you one step closer to success."**

# 100

## YOGYA DESU

# Strings of Passion: My Journey as a Violinist

### Finding My Voice Through Music

Hi, I'm Yogya Desu, and my greatest passion is music. Playing the violin isn't just a hobby for me - it's a way of expressing emotions and telling stories through melodies. From the moment I picked up the violin, I felt a deep connection to its strings, and that connection has grown stronger with each passing year.

### Achievements That Define Me

Through dedication and countless hours of practice, I have achieved:

- Multiple awards in violin competitions, recognizing both my technical precision and my emotional expression.

- Performances at prestigious venues, where I have had the honor of sharing my passion with a wider audience.

- Recognition for blending technical mastery with emotional storytelling, making each performance a memorable experience.

### Overcoming Challenges

Balancing intensive violin training with academics has been challenging, but with discipline and time management, I have been able to excel in both. There were moments of self-doubt, but each competition and performance has reinforced my belief in my abilities.

## The Role of 21K School

21K School has provided me with the freedom and flexibility to pursue my musical journey while excelling in academics. Without this support, balancing school and violin training would have been incredibly difficult.

## Looking to the Future

I dream of becoming a renowned violinist, sharing my music with the world and touching hearts through melodies.

To my fellow learners: **"Follow your passion, work hard, and never stop believing in yourself. Every note you play, every step you take, brings you closer to your dreams."**

# 101

# Zendagi Azad

# From Barriers to Breakthroughs: Afghan Story

## A Determined Beginning

Hi, I'm Zendagi Azad, a 14-year-old Grade 8 learner at 21K School. My journey has been one of resilience, hope, and the transformative power of education. Growing up in Afghanistan, I always valued learning. From kindergarten to Grade 6, I was an eager learner, participating in festivals, events, and academic activities. But everything changed when girls were banned from attending school. Suddenly, my access to education was taken away, and I was left wondering if I would ever be able to study again.

## Holding Onto Hope

When my school was shut down, I refused to let my love for learning fade away. I turned to English courses as a way to continue my education, despite the uncertain future. It wasn't easy - there were days filled with doubt and fear, but I held on to the dream of education. I kept imagining a future where learning was a right, not a privilege.

## A New Opportunity

My life took a turn when I learned about 21K School's scholarship program. Encouraged by my teacher, Miss Lubna, I applied, hoping for a chance to restart my education. The day I received my acceptance letter was one of the happiest moments of my life. Not only was I going back to school, but I was also stepping into a world of possibilities I had never imagined before.

## Achievements That Inspire Me

Since joining 21K School, I have flourished in my studies. Some of my proudest achievements include:

- Excelling in subjects like Coding, Chemistry, and Global Perspectives, where I explore real-world challenges and solutions.

- Working on an Interdisciplinary Project about Exoplanets, sparking my curiosity about space and scientific research.

- Discovering my artistic talent, using drawing as a form of self-expression and creativity.

- Creating a portrait of my friend, Manishka Dubey, which was a personal milestone in my journey of artistic growth.

## Overcoming Challenges

Transitioning from uncertainty to structured learning wasn't easy. I had to rebuild my confidence, manage my time effectively, and learn to study independently. But with support from my teachers, family, and the 21K School community, I adapted quickly. I found that education wasn't just about textbooks and exams - it was about critical thinking, self-expression, and believing in my potential.

## The Role of 21K School

21K School has been more than just an academic institution - it has been a gateway to a future I never thought possible. The flexibility of online learning allowed me to study from home while connecting with a global community of learners. My teachers encouraged me to explore my strengths, and for the first time in years, I felt like I was in control of my future.

## Looking to the Future

I now dream of a future where girls everywhere have access to education, where no one has to fight for the right to learn.

I aspire to contribute to the fields of science, technology, and global development, using knowledge to make a real impact.

To my fellow learners: **"No matter how difficult life may seem, there is always hope. Education is a light that can never be dimmed - keep striving, keep believing, and never give up on your dreams."**

www.ingramcontent.com/pod-product-compliance
Lightning Source LLC
Chambersburg PA
CBHW031548150726
47990CB00001B/267